THE
HIDDEN WORLD
OF
MISERICORDS

1. *Auch, Cathedral of Ste-Marie:* A section of the choir-stalls. The misericords can be seen at the lower part of the photograph, beneath the jutting ledges under the turned-up seats (Sixteenth Century).

THE
HIDDEN WORLD
OF
MISERICORDS

by Dorothy and Henry Kraus

GEORGE BRAZILLER, NEW YORK

PHOTOGRAPHIC CREDITS

The majority of the illustrations in this book were taken by Pascal Corbierre, Paris, who worked in close and faithful collaboration with the authors. This work was partly financed with the help of Elsa and Norman Yanover, to whom the authors extend their gratitude. Other photographic sources were: Archives Photographiques, Paris: Figs. 1, 3, 10, 54, 130; Hervé Seurat, Paris: 2; Stainacre, Pontarlier: 8, 62; Jon Naar, New York: 12, 60, 65; Syndicat d'Initiatif, Salins-les-Bains: 46; Friends of Lincoln Cathedral: 150; Chichester Cathedral postcard: 151; Victoria and Albert Museum: 152; D. T. Atkinson & Associates postcard: 153; Courtauld Photo Library, London: 154; Windsor Chapel brochure: 155; Institut Royal du Patrimoine Artistique, Brussels: 156, 157, 158, 159, 160, 161, 162; Foto Frenzel, Ulm: 163; Rheinisches Bildarchiv: 164; Bildarchiv-Foto Marburg: 165; *Mittelalterliches Chorgestuhl:* 166; Th. & H. Seeger, Basel: 167, 168; *Les stalles de l'insigne collegiale de St-Pierre et de St-Ours d'Aoste:* 169; The Map, "Misericords of France," was drawn by Wei-hsing Tu of Katz, Waisman and Weber, New York.

For information address the publisher:
George Braziller, Inc., One Park Avenue, New York, N.Y. 10016

Library of Congress Catalog Card Number: 75-10869
International Standard Book Number: 0-8076-0804-1

Printed in the U.S.A.
Designed by Christopher Simon, Simon-Erikson Associates

Contents

FOR MIRIAM,

whose humanity and wit
would have savored the quality
of the misericords.

Foreword

We have been waiting impatiently for the appearance of this book by Dorothy and Henry Kraus. There is, as they say, a hidden world of misericords, hidden because it has rarely been written about, hardly ever photographed.

Indeed, this world has been all but unknown to scholars themselves. The early writings on the subject by Louis Maeterlinck, the Belgian author, have been forgotten and are in fact outmoded. No general work on French underseat carvings has ever appeared.

Recently, a certain interest in them has begun to emerge in several countries. In books on popular imagery, authors have shown that themes of conjugal life, proverbs, or grotesques did not originate in the nineteenth century, as historians once believed, nor in the seventeenth century, as the savants of between-the-two-wars held, but far back in the Middle Ages: in the margins of illuminated manuscripts and in the misericords of the fourteenth century!

But their subject matter is not the sole feature that has stirred up this recent interest in the study of misericords. Of no less importance has been the realization of the extraordinary beauty and originality of these sculptures.

All the foregoing incited the authors to undertake, with verve and understanding, a vast survey of the misericords in French churches. Accompanied by a photographer and sparing neither time nor finance, they pursued their search into every corner of France with unflagging zeal.

For years, while this indefatigable effort continued, it was only their friends who knew about it, who could share with them the beauty and excitement of their discoveries. With the publication of their book this pleasure becomes accessible to a large audience, and the fascinating world of French misericords can now be appreciated by all, whether professional scholars or amateurs of art.

PROFESSOR JEAN ADHÉMAR
Curator-in-Chief, Bibliothèque Nationale
Editor, Gazette des Beaux-Arts

Preface

There is a mystery about the misericords of France. As abundant and beautiful as they are, they are scarcely known.

Aside from a few famous sets, scant attention has been paid them even by art specialists. There has never been a comprehensive book about them published in that country.

The French Ministry of Culture's registry, which is supposed to list every bit of old art in France's "patrimony," itself seems unaware of the treasure of the misericords.[1]

One of us worked in these files for several months and found underseat carvings cited on the average only once in twenty times at churches which, we subsequently learned, possessed them.

Our information came from local brochures, scattered articles, personal visits, and especially a mailed survey of a carefully selected list of five hundred churches. All added up to the fact that misericords do indeed exist in France.

They exist massively: almost eight thousand of them, in our still incomplete count, in every section of the country. And large numbers of them are of high quality.

France is not alone in this possession. Misericords are to be found almost everywhere in Europe, including the eastern countries. Italy, so rich in other art, seems least endowed in this field.[2]

The most notable collections outside of France are those of Belgium and Great Britain. The misericords of these countries have been catalogued, very recently—and excellently—in the latter.[3]

An illustrated section will be devoted at the end of the book to the collections in other countries.

In the aggregate, the study of misericords is still in its early stages, occupied mainly with what scientists call taxonomic matters such as discovery, identification, classification.

It is somehow consoling to think that the early botanists and horticulturists may have been drawn to their exhausting labors by the loveliness of flowers. We ourselves must confess that the task of collating underseat carvings and of searching out facts about them would not have tempted us were it not for the extraordinary beauty of the misericords.

D. and H. K.
Paris, November 1974

The Misericord as Object of Utility and Art

It is a hoary convention that art thrives on hardship. The art of the misericord was born out of indulgence.

The word *misericord* had a broad church usage. The book of rules of the famous old Parisian Abbey of St-Victor defined it as "anything allowed to an infirm person out of mercy." To the stern monastic world this might mean a glass of milk in the summer, an extra blanket in the winter, a bite of meat in the Lenten period, or, during the interminable offices carried out by night and day, permission to lean on a staff.

Sitting was not conceded until later, though at first only to the sick or feeble. With time, this limitation also was relaxed for certain parts of the offices. Even the rigorous Cistercians permitted occasional, selective sitting.[1]

As asceticism continued to recede, any remaining embarrassment about this indulgence was finally obviated by an ingenious invention. We hear of it in a document of 1121, where Pierre de Cluny, head of the renowned abbey, refers to *scabella* ("little seats") "attached to the seats."[2] They were no doubt underseat ledges on which the clerics could rest while they were ostensibly standing, their seat turned up. Their use strikes the modern mind as a naive self-deception. But the ledge won universal acceptance in the end, assuming the generic name of *misericord*.

Wood-carvers who fashioned the new type of seat arranged to do so from a single block. This permitted strengthening the jutting ledge by leaving a thickness of wood beneath it, which would then be neatly tapered off. The earliest seats-with-misericords have disappeared but we can safely assume that they were unadorned. Not for long, however, since almost everywhere in Europe examples still exist of thirteenth-century seats with carved misericords.[3]

We can only conjecture about how this sculpture began to be done. Contracts with artists are not available for the early period. All we do know is that suddenly such carvings surfaced in a hundred places like a new genus of botanical wonder.

Did the misericords reflect the medieval allergy to a bare surface? Were they meant to disguise the indulgent purpose of the ledge? We shall probably never know.

There is some evidence that the carving soon began to serve an identifying role. Canons, we know, were assigned permanent seats in the choir, paying for them when they assumed their posts. Some even marked them with their initials. How much more elegant to be able to say: "My seat is the one with the bagpipe-playing donkey on it!" This might avoid quarrels, besides, that could require the aid of the church *constabulari* in assigning places.[4]

Early misericords were carved simply with foliage or a stylized pattern. But their thematic scope developed swiftly, eventually taking on as broad a range as any to be found in medieval church art. Only the use of scriptural subjects was extremely sparse in the underseat carvings. Is the reason not obvious? The clerics were delicate about allowing the lower body to be in contact with the effigies of Christ, Mary, or the Apostles. This single circumstance had a fateful influence on the entire evolution of misericord imagery. It explains what many have found astonishing—that carved works done exclusively for the choir, the church's very heart, should assume a nonreligious, often even an irreverent, accent.

Our survey illustrates the degree and persistence of this trend. Of the nearly eight thousand misericords collated, only three percent have subjects drawn from scripture.[5] Since more than half of these are found in just two churches—Amiens and Auxerre Cathedrals—the voluntary taboo comes close to being universal.

Instead we find a body of subject matter that ranges over the entire gamut of medieval life: work scenes, professional occupations, daily activities, domestic subjects, human relationships, love, sex and pornography, portraiture, humor, recreation, games, music, dancing, animals.

Aside from a wide assortment of lively proverbial and folk-wisdom reference, there are relatively few derivative topics. Literary or allegorical sources that are readily recognizable are scarce. Foliar and floral carvings are most frequently represented in the misericords. Urban sculptors were still close to the soil and the Rouen canons could confidently expect faithful performance when ordering Laurent Isbré to produce "branches and clusters in the fashion of cabbage and thistle leaves."[6]

Underseat teratology is not very frightening, more often charming rather than hallucinatory. Both these and the botanical subjects are too extensive to have been included in the present survey. Misericord portraiture is often marked by its acute observation of character (Fig. 2). The prevailingly popular subjects depicted throb with intensity or are imbued with a voluntary exaggeration that links them to modern expressionism (Fig. 3).

For the churchmen, the banning of scriptural topics meant their virtual surrender of the role of initiating subject matter. It was not so much a question of their not caring to bother about misericord imagery. They simply were not equipped to compete with the secular offerings of the sculptors. While we must assume that the clerics did not give up their right of veto over the art of the misericords, it is nonetheless inescapable that their carvers were allowed a considerable license, greater, perhaps, than that enjoyed in any other area of church art.

Rigidly controlled, on the other hand, was most of the other sculpture of the stalls, such as the great upper statuary which is largely given over to apostles, saints, and prophets; or the aisle and terminal panel reliefs, usually devoted to scenes from the New Testament.

Authors who have tried to track down the origins of misericord imagery have searched in old literature, fabliaux, legends, manuscript and early bookprint illustration, missals, sermons, as well as in other art works. Their findings have been instructive but inevitably limited, for the humble background of the misericord-carvers reduced the availability to them of many of these cultural sources, resulting in their depending to a great extent on their own resources.

The art of the misericord-carvers was based essentially on life: the life they knew, the life they saw, the life they themselves lived. Even when they used derived sources they were inclined to adapt them freely. This occurred as much with proverbs and folk sayings, with which they were certainly familiar, as with more literary themes. Originality is one of the hallmarks of the misericords. It might be attained with a single deft touch, as in the frequent illustrations of what may be called foolish-act sayings. One of these is "The man who tries to shoe a goose." At St-Jean-de-Maurienne, the sculptor goes beyond the witless source to present a goose fully equipped with hooves and brandishing a horseshoe in its mouth.

It has been suggested that these modified interpretations were due to the carvers' misunderstanding of the

2. *Mozac, Church of St-Pierre:* Portrait of a Woman (Fifteenth Century).

3. *Church of St.-Pol-de-Léon:* Portrait of a Facial Paralytic (Sixteenth Century).

originals.[7] We feel, rather, that new ideas were often released by their fresh vision. At Rouen, "The man who tries to open his mouth as wide as an oven" is subtly changed to an alchemist with his scroll, calling out the magic formula to the flames.

Most often, the everyday source of the misericord is obvious and unadorned. The more than fifty occupations that we have found astonish by their variety and scrutinizing detail. Some of them have vanished, like the candlemaker, the fresh-water purveyor, or the bloodletter. But most others are still practiced today, wherever artisanry continues to resist mechanization.

France of the fifteenth and sixteenth centuries—when most of the finest misericords were made—was still overwhelmingly agricultural. That a relatively small number of work scenes in the misericords are rural marks the predominantly urban nature of this art. Most of it was created for cathedrals, important collegiate churches or town-based abbeys and monasteries.

Destruction of the misericords has been incalculable. The Revolution, which brought about the widespread dissolution of convents, was a major ravager. Fortunately, some of the misericords passed on to other churches.[8] The iconoclasm of the Huguenots, on the other hand, was usually irreversible.

Loss of misericords has continued into contemporary times. Modern wars have stripped several depart-

*All dates refer to stalls and/or misericords rather than to the churches in which they are located.

ments of the northeastern invasion routes almost entirely of their carvings.[9] A number of churches lost their sets in the last war; Rouen's was diminished by a fourth in a single bombing.

Neglect has also taken its toll. In our many visits to churches, we often found their misericords in a deplorable condition while thefts and unaccountable disappearances reported by curates have reduced other collections. At St-Martin-aux-Bois, once a great abbey church now abandoned to the swifts, a tornado in the mid-nineteenth century had blown out part of the vault, which remained unrepaired for decades. The mold that attacked the beautiful stallwork has now reached an advanced state.

High on the list of destroyers of misericords were the churchmen themselves. Starting at the end of the seventeenth century, this vandalism was part of the widespread movement to "bring light" into the churches. One important phase was the opening up of choirs. Did the clerics suddenly become self-conscious about the art contained in their heretofore private world? What is inescapable is that with few exceptions misericords that were done thereafter are without much interest, a succession of repeated angel heads, masks, or floral designs.

It has been said that churchmen paid little attention to the misericords, and that this explains the frequent coarseness and even obscenity of their subjects. Such a view does little justice to the lusty-mindedness of the early clerics. Certainly it would have been strange if they persisted in paying for work that shocked or disgusted them.

A similar error has led to the belief that the misericords are often anti-clerical. This view ignores the various divisions of the medieval church, which only in dogma was firmly monolithic. Competition for donations and bequests was at times extremely bitter, the success of the late-coming Mendicants proving particularly infuriating to the established groups. This accounts for the frequency of scenes, ostensibly innocent annotations from the fabled "Reynard," showing a fox or wolf, often cowled, preaching to a flock of hens or geese, one of which may already be stowed away in his hood. The friars are actually aimed at.

This subject attains an extravagant form at Mortain, where a robber-monk is seen fleeing from a mill with a bag of meal, aided by a demon. Yet even this scene could hardly compare with the virulent commentary in a misericord at St. George's Chapel of Windsor Castle, where a friar is shown evacuating a devil whom other monks and demons are busily molding to diabolic perfection.

A considerable number of stall donors are known. Churchmen lead the list but one sees also kings and princes and high nobles among them. What is more surprising is to find burghers quite frequently helping to furnish the clerics' private world, which suggests that it was not always as hermetical as has been supposed. This surmise becomes a certainty in the case of the collegiate church of Villefranche-de-Rouergue, where the singular privilege of occupying places in the stalls granted to eight of the city's leading laymen assumes a patronage role.

In the second part of this book, where a number of France's finest sets of misericords are grouped, the variety of patrons responsible for them is illustrated. Studied, too, are ways in which this donorship may have influenced the subject matter and even the style of the carvings.

The master-artisan of the great stalls of the Cathedral of St-Claude was so highly esteemed that his kneeling effigy was carved on a large panel, where he is shown receiving the blessings of the church's patron saint. His great compass hangs at his belt and his name is prominently inscribed: Jehan de Vitry (Fig. 4). We know of no similar consecration extended to a maker of stalls in France though the name of "Jan Trupin" is gracefully carved on Amiens's splendid set in two places (Fig. 5).

xii

4. *St-Claude, Cathedral of St-Pierre:* Portrait of Jehan de Vitry, master-builder of the choir-stalls (Fifteenth Century).

5. *Amiens, Cathedral of Notre-Dame:* Carved Inscription of Jan Trupin, one of the sculptors who worked on the choir-stalls (Sixteenth Century).

Assumed self-portraits, without inscriptions, are more abundant, the ascription usually taking the form of the artist holding up the misericord ledge. At Rouen, a misericord that was destroyed in the 1944 bombing presented a sculptor with a chisel, putting in the last strokes on a figure—on a misericord!

The names of many carvers who worked on choirstalls are known. More than one hundred fifty of them at some sixty churches were listed in the documents and literature that we consulted. This extensive roster is far from complete.[10]

Invidious views are sometimes offered that sculpting misericords was considered of minor importance, shunned by "the most distinguished carvers, except, perhaps, during their apprentice years."[11] Greater consideration is of course extended to the upper-stall sculpture by such critics. Yet the documents rarely make a distinction about the part on which artists worked. That the finest among them often exerted their talents on the underseat carving is patent, however, in the extraordinary skill that characterizes so much of it. Such was, indeed, the proven case of Pol Mosselmen, a Fleming who worked on Rouen's stalls, receiving top billing in the fabric's *Comptes* (accounts) as "sculptor of statues." He signed one contract, on July 28, 1458, to do "24 apostles" and "24 angels" for the upper stalls, for example.[12]

But the same parchment also called for six "ymages" for the "sellettes," that is, the misericords, for which Mosselmen was to receive thirty *sous*. In another document, of February 28, 1532, a "sculptor of images" working on the stalls of Troyes Cathedral is similarly shown to have been paid for the carving of the "sellettes."[13]

Stall carvers were usually referred to as *huchers* (wood-carvers) or simply carpenters or joiners. The modest references tend to be misleading since these men developed high skills while making elegant furniture or doing ornamental decorative and figure carving on wooden houses.

In the contracts that have survived, fees are frequently mentioned. It is impossible to construct any kind of pattern from them because of the chaotic differences in medieval money values as well as the frequent addition of bonuses and perquisites or partial payment in the form of food, drink, and lodging. Also, either party may have been required to supply the wood and other materials.

Total cost varied greatly, besides, in accordance with the magnitude and complexity of the job. It seems appropriate, nevertheless, that the fabulous set at Amiens, whose one hundred ten misericords (originally one hundred twenty) are encrusted in stalls of extraordinary splendor, should have recorded the highest cost of all those known in France, nearly 9,500 *livres.*

At Saumur, a problem of compensation with a peculiarly modern twist developed when two carvers, who had agreed to do the stalls at so much a seat, abandoned the task after a year, finding that they had "lost money on the original contract." A new group was hired, to be paid by the day, which was considered more equitable. Yet in the end, these men completed the job at a considerable saving to their employers.[14]

The position and use of the misericord imposed certain stringent conditions on its carvers, which have been the source of ingenious adaptations. The narrow horizontality of the space resulted in the frequent use of reclining, kneeling, seated, or bowed positions, which are usually very artfully arranged.

The extreme exiguity of the carving field—less than a foot square on the average—forced the reduction of the number of figures used to a minimum. This put a sharp test on the sculptor's story-telling capacity, but the resulting simplification often heightened its effectiveness as well as that of the overall design. The latter is at times enriched by cubistic tussocks or toothed granitic clusters that may give it a surrealistic aspect.

Hard usage rendered even the toughest oak or chestnut, the woods most commonly used for the misericords, subject to frequent breakage. High-relief carving was, hence, usually avoided, the sculptor giving salient elements positional distortions that are sometimes ludicrous, frequently charming, and in the main wonderfully adept.

Above all, it was the freedom of the medieval misericord-maker's work that was its most distinctive feature. It also resulted in a kind of anarchy. Since clerics rarely had a role in initiating subject matter, interrelated "programs" are almost unknown among the underseat carvings.

Instead, the subjects of any set usually have a haphazard quality, each carving living a separate life, without organic relationship other than style to its neighbors.

But the preoccupations of the sculptors, however widely dispersed the sites of their activity, were remarkably homogeneous, reflecting the basic human interests and activities with which they were concerned.

Some of this related thematic material has been joined together in the section that follows, offering a more revealing vision than any available in a single place of the remarkable world that lies hidden beneath the choir-stall seats.

ICONOGRAPHIC
PATTERNS

Mating

Though with intermittent relapses, the harsh monastic ethic was losing its authority by the fifteenth century. Nowhere in church art was this more apparent than in the misericords and in no area more strikingly than in the relationship of the sexes.

While marriage was still upheld as the divinely ordained state for man and woman, the choir's underseat carvings did not exclude other possibilities of felicity. However delicately handled, sex remained the central fact of their bond though it might be disguised as a Picasso-type of obsessive love of an old satyr for a young nymph or presented in the surrogate form of two amative animals.

The latter might have been imagined by the artists to be the actual description of the amorous life of the earth's other creatures, whether apes, turtles, frogs, even serpents, or that great aviary of coupling members of the feathered tribe.

But at times the limits of nature are strained beyond misreading; the disguise is shattered by the very perfection of the symbolism. And we can no longer escape the true, intended meaning of the adoring snails.

6. The Wedding Band (Fifteenth Century). *St-Jean-de-Maurienne, Cathedral of St-Jean-Baptiste.*

7. The Lovers (Fifteenth Century). *Church of St-Chamant.*

8. The Flower People (Sixteenth Century). *Church of Montbenoît.*

9. The Proposal (Sixteenth Century). *St-Bertrand-de-Comminges, Church of Notre-Dame.*

10. The Shared Bath (Sixteenth Century). *Paris, Church of St-Gervais-St-Protais.*

11. A Dancing Couple (Sixteenth Century). *Paris, Church of St-Gervais-St-Protais.*

12. The Adoring Snails (Sixteenth Century). *Mantes-la-Jolie, Church of Gassicourt.*

The Daughters of Eve

Man's expulsion from the Garden was long reverberant in his consciousness, as was the thought that it was the woman—Eve—who was to blame.

Were he to forget for a moment this bitter legacy, it would be brought back to him by a hundred foils, not the least of which were his curate's sermons.

That woman could not be sculpted without the Devil's aid was a concept redolent of the cloister, which tended always to associate the monks' two most dangerous foes.

But the medieval layman, and the misericord carver who expressed his thoughts, did not veer very much from this misogynous view, blaming woman's inherent desire to shear man's strength, like Delilah, or to ride him as Campaspe did great Aristotle's crawling figure as the price of her favors.

An astonishing modern note is struck in the misericords by "the fight for the culottes," which Freudians might ascribe to penis-envy and in which the woman was expected to be victorious. Indeed, that is the outcome of every family squabble depicted in them. At best, woman was an incorrigible scold, man her long-suffering victim.

The mortal sin of Unchastity is always illustrated by a woman in the misericords. At Caen, as a latter-day Venus, she reclines with her abbreviated skirt accenting her charms like a girl on exhibition in a brothel.[1] Looking directly at the viewer, she addresses a kind of illustrated sermon to him. Pointing one finger up to heaven, another down to hell, she lays out for him the extremes of man's experience with sex, of which her own lustful body is both the object and the scourge.

13. Woman, Creation of the Devil (Fifteenth Century). *Church of St-Martin-aux-Bois.*

14. Aristotle Paying for the Favors of the Courtesan Campaspe (Fifteenth Century). *Rouen, Cathedral of Notre-Dame.*

15.   Samson and Delilah (Sixteenth Century). *Church of Villabé.*

16. The Fight for the Culottes (Fifteenth Century). *Rouen, Cathedral of Notre-Dame.*

17.   The Vice of Unchastity (Seventeenth Century). *Caen, Church of St-Etienne.*

The Comforts of Life

That Frenchmen and Frenchwomen of the fifteenth and sixteenth centuries depicted in the misericords were much concerned about food and drink should occasion no surprise.

The habit is still with them.

It is far more unexpected to find a man and a woman sharing the task of washing up the dishes after a meal, as in the carving at Rouen. Modern French husbands have been liberated from such chores!

A warm fire, a bath—the latter·not precluding visitors—were other appreciated amenities. Or sleep: commoners can be seen stretching out anywhere for a siesta or simply dropping their heads onto their knees.

All these placid scenes could cause us to forget the extent to which medieval life was marked by violence. But the underseat carvings themselves do not permit such an error. Fisticuffs and swordplay have more than an ample part in them.

Even the poor had their share of pleasure, though it was often on the purely negative side, like the removal of a pebble from a peasant's shoe!

18. The Shared Task: Dishwashing (Fifteenth Century). *Rouen, Ca-thedral of Notre-Dame.*

19. The Drinker (Sixteenth Century). *Puy-Notre-Dame, Church of Notre-Dame.*

20. Man Warming Himself at a Fireplace (Fifteenth Century). *Ven-dôme, Church of La Trinité.*

21. Man in the Tub, with Visitor (Fifteenth Century). *Sougé, Church of St-Quentin.*

22. Peasant Emptying Pebble from His Shoe (Fifteenth Century).
Flavigny-sur-Ozerain, Church of St-Genest.

Urban Trades and Occupations

Only the stained-glass lancets can compare with the misericords as depictors of city trades and crafts, which appear in the donor panels of guild-given windows of many churches.

Nothing permits us to assume, however, that the great number of work scenes presented in the underseat carvings are crediting "signatures" of guild or confraternity donors. Yet everything suggests that their presence was not due to accident or whim, either.

Their existence in so many church collections hints at some particular relationship between the tradesmen depicted and the clerics. The uniqueness of a number of the crafts also has the gauge of authenticity. And the extraordinary care with which they were done, the meticulous attention paid to work implements and methods, indicate that the critical eye of practitioners oversaw their making.

All the needs of medieval man are provided by the more than fifty trades that are carved on the collated misericords: food, drink, clothing, shelter, heating, home furnishings, utensils, and the transporters and purveyors that go with them.

Nor are the liberal professions or the luxury or entertainment crafts forgotten, nor even the servants that only the rich could afford. In the main, however, the trades of basic necessity are stressed, as befits the profoundly popular world of the misericords.

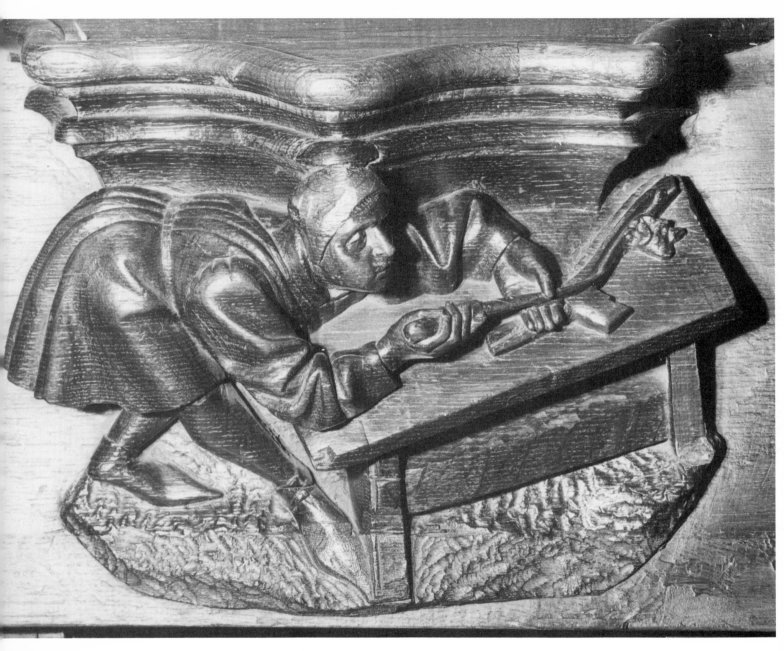

23. The Wood-Carver (Fifteenth Century). *Rouen, Cathedral of Notre-Dame.*

24. The Baker (Sixteenth Century). *Church of Estouteville-Ecalles.*

25. The Cook (Sixteenth Century). *Bordeaux, Church of St-Seurin.*

26. **The Blacksmith (Fifteenth Century).** *Basilica of St-Denis, formerly at Abbey of St-Lucien-de-Beauvais.*

27.   The Boatmen (Fifteenth Century). *St-Claude, Cathedral of St-Pierre.*

28. The Money-Lender (Fifteenth Century). *Rouen, Cathedral of Notre-Dame.*

29.   The Teacher (Sixteenth Century). *Auxerre, Cathedral of St-Etienne.*

Work on the Land

There is an old tradition in church art of picturing farm occupations, known as "The Labors of the Months." Stemming from the Romans, who designated in this way the eternal round of the seasons, the Middle Ages developed the idea into a typical Christian concept: redemption through work.

Misericord portrayals of farm work were inevitably influenced by this tradition. Yet originality as always brightened these carvings, whether by the introduction of new subjects or reinterpretation of the old.

May is a hunter; torrid August a young man hurrying out to the fields with a pitcher of refreshing wine. There is humor in one faceless reaper and surprise in another, who turns out to be a woman, the sex, too, of the apple-pickers at Rouen. October's wine-making scene shows one man already nailing down a barrel whereas his companion is only at the grape-treading stage, enjoying meanwhile a bunch of the prefermented fruit.

Church art generally contents itself for November's pig-killing scene with the symbolic lifting of an axe above the placid acorn-gobbler. But at Vendôme the peasant straddles the overturned animal and plunges his knife with zest into its jugular.

One halts in delight at the unusual scene of the beehive workers until one realizes that one has seen it before, on a twelfth-century stone capital from the Abbey of Vezelay. Some scholars contended that it represented there the Four Rivers of Paradise. Now we know, in any case, how the misericord carvers read it.

30.   The Sower (Sixteenth Century). *Champeaux, Church of St-Martin.*

31.   The Reaper (Sixteenth Century). *Church of Boos.*

32. The Apple-Pickers (Fifteenth Century). *Rouen,
Cathedral of Notre-Dame.*

33. The Hunter: Month of May (Fifteenth Century). *Vendôme, Church of La Trinité.*

34. Wine-Making: Month of October (Fifteenth Century). *Vendôme, Church of La Trinité.*

35. Killing the Fatted Pig: Month of November (Fifteenth Century). *Vendôme, Church of La Trinité.*

36. The Bee-Keepers (Fifteenth Century). *Paris, Cluny Museum, formerly at Abbey of St-Lucien-de-Beauvais.*

Wise Words and Foolish Acts

You will not find in misericord proverbs that type of popular manual of agronomy by which peasants used to arrange their chores, telling them when to plant and when to gather and whether a fat or a lean winter was in view. Such advice was not pertinent to townsfolk.

The fifteenth century was too early, on the other hand, for the Ben Franklin kind of storekeeper's wisdom that celebrated diligence and thrift.

Misericord proverbs were an invitation to laughter, their wise counsel usually bypassed and only the hilarious consequences recorded: a man beating his brains out on a brick wall or trying to propel a windmill with his breath or falling between two chairs.

Medieval man's love of fun extended to the point of an engaging willingness to be ridiculous himself, which crested in yearly extravaganzas like the Festival of Fools, echoes of which appear repeatedly in the carvings.

But the sculptor in his disregard for handed-down meanings might at times willfully alter a message, like the one that tells us that "Two dogs gnawing one bone seldom agree." At Vendôme, he is seen intervening forthrightly on the side of justice to help a starved cur get his fair share of the meal.

37. "Small Rain Calms Big Wind" (Translation of one facet of pun: "Petite Pluie Abat Grand Vent") (Sixteenth Century). *Champeaux, Church of St-Martin.* (See Note 1, Champeaux.)

38.   "To Fill a Purse with Air" (Sixteenth Century).
Presles, Church of St-Germain.

39.   "To Shoe a Goose" (Fifteenth Century). *Church of St-Martin-aux-Bois.*

40. Flemish Proverb, "He Shits Eggs Without Shells" (Fifteenth Century).
Bordeaux, Church of St-Seurin.

41. "Two Dogs on One Bone," with Man Taking Sides (Fifteenth Century). *Vendôme, Church of La Trinité.*

The Carnival Spirit

The invariability of man's amusements is often invoked as comment to Peter Brueghel's famous painting of games. But the Flemish artist did not invent these sports, he merely recorded them. Misericord carvers did the same, some hundred years or more before Brueghel's time.

We are sometimes struck, nonetheless, by certain alterations in the way these sports are played today. Some of the changes were no doubt due to the systematization occasioned by modern professionalism.

Personal tests of physical strength were popular in underseat carving, as they must have been in medieval life. Also, the posturings of the waning knight class were satirized in sham contests, the rivals even being mounted on hobbyhorses! No more serious were the fierce-looking swordplay acts at the fairs, which featured a gamut of other entertainments as well.

Halloween-type masquerades were institutionalized in the Festival of Fools, an allowed annual license from discipline's rigidities, which was marked by extravagant merrymaking, mock masses, and fools' bishops.[2]

42. Shuttlecock (Sixteenth Century). *Champeaux, Church of St-Martin.*

43.   A Game of Cricket (Sixteenth Century). *Champeaux, Church of St-Martin.*

44. Sword-Play at the Fair (Fifteenth Century). *Vendôme, Church of La Trinité.*

45. The Double-Jointed Man (Sixteenth Century). *Tréguier, Cathedral of St-Tugdual.*

46. The Fools' Bishop (Sixteenth Century). *Salins-les-Bains, Church of St-Anatoile.*

Music and Dancing

Music is the most sacred of the arts and is often heard in Heaven. Its action is considered so tonic, indeed, that its practice is not confined to the angels but is granted to all God's creatures, including even the animals.

Men and beasts usually play the noisier, commoner types of instruments in the misericords: bagpipes and drums and things that are blown. An exception is the organ, of which the ass is master, a fun-poking hand-me-down from the fabliaux. The angel musicians themselves may at times lack the ethereal spirit, looking like transvestized choir boys at Rogation's-tide and may even be carved without their wings, as occurs with one angel-musician at Le Mans.

Dancing occurs more rarely. It was frowned on by clerics and was often shown in other church art to be devil-inspired, leading women to loose acts and perdition. In the underseat carvings, however, it appears as one of the permitted excesses of the Festival of Fools.

The church's condemnation of dancing had a kind of negative scriptural sanction: it is rarely found in the Gospels and then most pejoratively. In the Old Testament, it occurs far more often, in celebration of victories and other memorable events.

Such an ascription may well be applicable to the handsome dancing man with the oriental turban and earrings in the carving at St-Cernin. For did not King David go into a hectic terpsichorean whirl to avert God's anger while the holy ark was being brought back to the tabernacle (II Samuel 6)?[3]

47.   The Dancing Bears (Fifteenth Century). *Church of St-Martin-aux-Bois.*

48.   The Angel Flute-Player (Sixteenth Century). *Le Mans, Cathedral of St-Julien.*

49. The Flageolet-Player (Seventeenth Century). *Caen, Church of St-Etienne.*

50.   Musician Tuning His Lute (Fifteenth Century). *Church of St-Chamant.*

51. The Bagpipe-Player (Fifteenth Century). *Rouen, Cathedral of Notre-Dame.*

52. A Family of Musicians (Fifteenth Century). *Paris, Cluny Museum, formerly at Abbey of St-Lucien-de-Beauvais.*

53. King David as Dancer (Fifteenth Century). *Church of St-Cernin, formerly at St-Chamant.*

The Animal Kingdom

It was difficult for medieval man to see animals in the purity of their nature. Moralistic preconceptions, stemming from the old Christian bestiaries, transmuted them into thinly veiled symbols of the vices and virtues or parabolic homilies on man's destiny. The serpent recalled the horror of man's initial error; the blind owl represented the Jews' hardnecked refusal to see Christ's truth; the kneeling camel figured Jesus' willingness to take on man's sinful burden.

But the untrammeled vision of the misericord sculptor and his comparative freedom from dogmatic sway helped him at times to overcome such conceptual deformations and to grasp the true charm and uniqueness of earth's other creatures.

As for the animals portrayed in humor, their role throughout the ages has been that of human substitutes, disguised as asses, bears, pigs, monkeys. They are no different in the misericords.

We see the primates particularly as pre-Darwinian facsimiles of evolved man, educated apes making love, reading from a lectern, churning butter, turning a spit, threading yarn, robbing a purse, examining a vial of urine, or administering a clyster.

54.   The Serpent (Fifteenth Century). *Prey, Church of Notre-Dame.*

55. Two Horses (Sixteenth Century). *St-Bertrand-de-Comminges, Church of Notre-Dame.*

56. Dog Attacking Rabbit (Fifteenth Century). *St-Claude, Cathedral of St-Pierre.*

57. **The Cat as Domestic Animal (Fifteenth Century).** *Paris, Cluny Museum, formerly at Abbey of St-Lucien-de-Beauvais.*

58. Monkey Administering a Clyster (Fifteenth Century). *Ville-franche-de-Rouergue, Collegiate Church of Notre-Dame.*

The World of Religion

While the misericords were largely inspired by secular thought and being, the immense role that systematized religion played in medieval life is inevitably reflected in a number of the carvings.[4] These consist of angels, saints, priests, prelates, clerical orders and activities, sermons, sacraments, worshippers, pilgrims, and a great assortment of Christian symbolism.

Underseat sculpture was, as might be expected, little concerned with philosophical concepts except for the occasional warning by means of death's heads and incised legends that "We All Must Die."

As in all other types of religious art, the vices have a more colorful delineation in the misericords than their opposites, showing up best in violent confrontations between the two.

Underseat carvers found their greatest verve when handling the Devil's team: demons and sorceresses and heretics.

Depiction of heterodoxy found a burning topicality in the sixteenth century in the guise of Protestantism, so mortal a danger at the time when many of the finest misericords were being carved.[5]

59.   The Triumph of Good over Evil (Sixteenth Century). *Church of Estoute ville-Ecalles.*

60. The Sermon (Sixteenth Century). *Mantes-la-Jolie, Church of Gassicourt.*

61. The Flagellant (Sixteenth Century). *Bourg-en-Bresse, Eglise de Brou.*

62. The Hypocrite at Prayer (Sixteenth Century). *Church of Montbenoît.*

63. The Sorceress (Fifteenth Century). *Solignac, Church of St-Pierre.*

64. The Jewish Owl Pecked at by Christian Birds (Fifteenth Century). *Les Andelys, Church of Notre-Dame.*

65. The Rats of Heresy Gnawing at the Christian World (Sixteenth Century). *Mantes-la-Jolie, Church of Gassicourt.*

THE
OUTSTANDING FRENCH
COLLECTIONS

Wine-Merchants and Apothecaries

Nowhere is the mortality of misericords better illustrated than at Paris, where but one church, St-Gervais, still possesses its early choir-stall carvings. A dozen others are known to have had misericords, among them the once famous Abbey of St-Victor,[1] some of whose surviving pieces have been rediscovered in recent times in widely scattered places,[2] all of them subjects from the Old Testament.

Authors have claimed that even St-Gervais's set has had an outside provenance, coming supposedly from Port-Royal, after that nunnery had fallen into the hands of the heretical Jansenists and was abolished in 1710.[3] But a scrutiny of the misericords will reveal the error of this attribution.

Their often risqué subjects, which sometimes graze the scatological, could hardly have been made for Cistercian nuns. Alien to a rural monastery, besides, would have been the many artisans and tradesmen depicted under the St-Gervais seats. Most of these occupations are known to have been practiced in St-Gervais's parish in earlier times.[4] Their guilds and confraternities were active at the church, participating in its building and decorating operations. Included were wine-merchants, apothecaries, architects and boatmen, all of whom are figured on the misericords.

The wine-wholesalers' confraternity, for example, was established at St-Gervais in 1343, shortly after Paris's wine unloading port was shifted to a quay hardly a hundred meters from the church. It founded its own chapel there, in which a daily mass was sung at an early hour to accommodate members who had to go to work betimes.

Most of St-Gervais's misericords have suffered badly from mutilation. From the character of the disfigurement it is evident that this was not the work of a layman's hand but rather of some prudish clergyman's. Hacked almost beyond recognition is the apothecary at his once much-appreciated task of relieving a patient (probably a woman) with a clyster. Equally mauled is the young man defecating before his girl friend's house, which was supposed to be a sovereign method of winning her favors.

Somehow, the mutilation that strikes us as most outrageous is that of a couple sharing a bath, a popular pastime of that era (see Fig. 10). Chopping away at the young woman's naked form, the iconoclast no doubt intended to ruin it beyond recognition.

But art's magic presents the ravaged pair to us as whole and true as life. The charming scene breathes a defiant innocence. She waits serenely for her husband or lover to join her, reaching a welcoming hand toward him as he extends his own to her cheek for a soft caress. Beyond all defacement, this misericord remains one of the loveliest underseat carvings in France.

An additional misericord from St-Gervais: Fig. 11.

66. The Architect and His Assistant (Sixteenth Century). *Paris, Church of St-Gervais-St-Protais.*

67. The Wine-Merchant (Sixteenth Century). *Church of St-Gervais-St-Protais.*

68. The Master Shoemaker (Sixteenth Century). *Church of St-Gervais-St-Protais.*

69. Creation of the Birds and Fishes (Sixteenth Century). *Church of Les Bottereaux, formerly at the Abbey of St-Victor, Paris.*

70. Creation of the Heavenly Bodies (Sixteenth Century). *Church of Les Bottereaux, formerly at the Abbey of St-Victor, Paris.*

The Defiant Churchmen

Preservation of St-Martin-de-Champeaux's fascinating misericords was the favor of a stubborn canonic disobedience. Yet the order for their suppression, issued in 1787 by the highest archdiocesan authority, was formal, precise, apparently inexorable.

What made the mandate particularly serious was the fact that it was issued pursuant to a pastoral visit that the prelate had just made to the collegiate church, where he had evidently examined its misericords in mounting horror and two hundred sixty-five years after their making discovered their iniquity.

From his archiepiscopal palace at Paris adjoining Notre-Dame, Monsignor du Juigné dictated his decree: "(We) exhort the canons of Champeaux and nevertheless enjoin them to arrange to change, and with the least delay, the bizarre and singular figures that can be seen on their stalls."[1]

We do not know what went on at Champeaux's capitular session following the receipt of this edict. But the final decision was a shrewd bit of labyrinthine diplomacy in which medieval churchmen were so adept. The canons chose to misunderstand the order. Instead of destroying the offensive carvings they had them painted an ugly ochre color, as if their spiritual attractiveness and not their physical existence were in question.

One is at a loss today to understand what it was about the misericords that so agitated the archbishop. Surely it could not have been the twelve delightful carvings that tell the full story of Job or the many others that glorify Christian virtue and Catholic orthodoxy.

He may have objected, it is true, to the piece showing a man pissing lustily against a large threshing basket, a punning rendition of the proverb: "Small rain calms big wind" (see Fig. 37).[2] Or the few innocent devilries among the carvings may have affronted him. But why destroy all because of a handful?

Some works of art seem wefted with a magical protective essence. Champeaux's fifty-four misericords could have been ravaged a dozen times after their carving, in 1522, by Richard Falaise, a Paris joiner, who was paid 450 livres for his work.[3]

The once prosperous town was often invaded and pillaged, finally by the Huguenots in 1652, who set fire to the church, destroying its vestments and papers and even its portal, which was never restored. But the stalls were unhurt.

With the Revolution came a moment when the church itself teetered on the brink, after its canons were dispersed. But St-Martin and its misericords were once more spared. And there they are today, all of them, with their wide range of theme and action.

One of the most arresting pieces is cloaked in mystery, presenting a person, possibly a woman,[4] with wide-open eyes, extended on an anvil. At her head and feet are two men with heavy hammers, one young, one old, prepared to strike. Is she alive? Is she dead? Is she a woman at all or rather just a symbolic figure, forever impenetrable to man and hence inimical?

Other misericords from Champeaux: Figs. 30, 42, and 43.

71.   God Challenged by the Devil to Put Job to the Test (Sixteenth Century).
Champeaux, Church of St-Martin.

72.   Job Ridiculed by His Wife (Sixteenth Century).
Champeaux, Church of St-Martin.

73. God Bearing the Burden of the World (Sixteenth Century). *Champeaux, Church of St-Martin.*

74. The Woman on the Anvil (Sixteenth Century). *Champeaux, Church of St-Martin.*

Hunt of the Artichoke-Gobbler

Tréguier's carving is a revealing example of the gap between an art patron's specifications and their realization. When St-Tugdual's canons felt too crowded in their old stall-seats and in 1508 ordered new ones made, the art called for in the contract that was drawn up simply mentioned "foliages" and "grimaces" (meaning monsters).

Performance of the carvers must have been satisfactory since gratifications to Gérard Dru and Tugdual Kergus were over 10 percent of the 773 livres they received. Part of the gratuities offered them were in the form of an "honest" burial spot in the cathedral, but the men said they would prefer something more substantial "at the present time."[1]

Foliages and monsters there are, indeed, among Tréguier's misericords. But there is much else, besides. There is, for example, a good deal of humor, rough and raucous. No wonder that the revolutionaries who tore through the cathedral in 1794 with their racking hatchets left the underseat carvings absolutely intact.

Inspiration for many of St-Tugdual's forty-six misericords came straight from the noisy, vital city. Brittany's leading commercial center, it alone enjoyed the "right of bourgeoisie" in the sixteenth century. Ocean trade was Tréguier's major industry, its boats plying the Channel and the Atlantic to England, Spain, and Portugal.

Dru and Kergus needed but a word or two to set their imaginative chisels going. But what came out in the end could hardly have been foreseen by the patrons. Part of our own surprise is due to a deficit of historic background, no doubt. One never suspected, for example, that there were mines and miners in Brittany in the sixteenth century. However—alerted by a misericord—a record was discovered showing that the city's port handled almost a thousand tons of wine and *iron* in the year of 1539–1540, in seventeen voyages by one group of twelve ships, all of which were named after their captains' wives.[2]

It does not, on the other hand, surprise us to find botanical subjects among the misericords, since they were so common among underseat carvings. But what does astonish and delight us is to recognize among them the flower of an artichoke![3]

Even today, Brittany is France's major producer of this tasty if niggardly tuber. It must have been as highly prized then as it is now, by the field parasites as well as by man. We learn as much from another scene, strange and hallucinatory, that looks like nothing more than a sainted hero fighting a dragon.

Actually, the latter is a kind of caterpillar gnawing away at the fruit of an artichoke. But we see the worm through the peasant's inflamed vision, enormously magnified into the delineaments of a monster, as the poor man goes about in his nightmare with a great club hunting the gobbler of his precious crop.

Another misericord from Tréguier: Fig. 45.

75.   The Miner (Sixteenth Century). *Tréguier, Cathedral of St-Tugdual.*

76. The Flower of the Artichoke (Sixteenth Century).
Tréguier, Cathedral of St-Tugdual.

77. Hunt of the Artichoke-Gobbler (Sixteenth Century).
Tréguier, Cathedral of St-Tugdual.

78.   Rear Exposure (Sixteenth Century). *Tréguier, Cathedral of St-Tugdual.*

79. The Glutton (Sixteenth Century). *Tréguier, Cathedral of St-Tugdual.*

The Labors of the Months

Sparing of the misericords by Tréguier's revolutionaries was by no means exceptional. The same occurred in many other churches. The militants saw no harm in these carvings, little that could be castigated as "art of feudalism and superstition."

The greatest loss of misericords during this period was due to the shutting down of monastic establishments. The men of '89 had no particular affection for the stall carvings, either. When Vendôme's abbey church was disestablished in 1790, the best they could suggest for its grandiose choir furniture was that it be sold "for firewood."[1] Instead, a master carpenter acquired the great wooden structure with the idea of earning an honest *sou* from it. Making the rounds of small village parishes, where the revolutionary winds blew less ardently, he disposed piecemeal of La-Trinité's eighty-eight magnificent fifteenth-century stalls.

After the restoration of the cult at Vendôme, the nostalgia for the former glory of its choir-stalls started a protracted search among nearby country churches. By 1835, thirty-two of the original set were reintegrated at the Trinité; the rest are still unaccounted for.

Despite the loss of almost two of every three of its misericords, what remains at La-Trinité-de-Vendôme is sufficient to give an impression of the former amplitude and imaginativeness of its collection. Originality is its brassard. For example, eight remaining pieces help us to identify the only set of Labors of the Months we have found among the French misericords.

Aside from October's wine-making and November's pig-killing scenes, each so novel (see Figs. 34 and 35), May is presented exceptionally as a hunter, June as a sheepshearer, and July as a young peasant bringing refreshments out to the field-workers.

The appearance at La-Trinité of this imagery of the countryside is perfectly understandable in view of the abbey's great landed holdings, owned from very early times, which were spread over fifteen priories.[2]

Among the other varied subjects treated in the misericords, there is one which has always been identified simply as "two beggars" but which more likely had a topical reference. For the Trinité was until the Revolution the possessor, preserved in a vial, of the sacred "Holy Tear" that Christ was supposed to have dropped on Lazarus's grave.

Since the eleventh century, when Geoffroy Martel, Count of Anjou, had acquired this miracle-working relic for the abbey, it had been the annual goal of thousands of blind pilgrims. Like the two old men of our carving, hopeful of a cure, they came to press their lips to the holy reliquary on "Lazarus's Friday."

Other misericords from Vendôme: Figs. 20, 33–35, 41 and 44.

80. Snail Nibbling at a Leaf (Fifteenth Century). *Vendôme, Church of La Trinité.*

81. Trimming the Vine: Month of March (Fifteenth Century). *Vendôme, Church of La Trinité.*

82. The Candlemaker (Fifteenth Century). *Vendôme, Church of La Trinité.*

83. Blind Pilgrims on "Lazarus's Friday" (Fifteenth Century). *Vendôme, Church of La Trinité.*

The Beast in Man

Though the identity of those who paid for the creation of stalls (and hence the misericords) is quite frequently known, this does not always help us to make a link between them and the subject matter. Usually the patrons seem to have played little part in the choice of themes, to say nothing of interpretation and style.

Different was the case at St-Pierre, the most important church of Saumur, where we not only know the donors but can observe their influence on the carvings as well. They were a militant group of pious action with a rather forbidding name: *Brothers and Sisters of the Confraternity of Priests Founded in Honor of the Altar of the Holy Sacrament.*[1]

St-Pierre's misericords were carved in 1474–1478, shortly following the apocalyptic Hundred Years' War, a period marked by two opposite tendencies. One was a surge of grateful piety; the other an abandonment to hedonistic pleasure, of which Saumur was a notorious example.

By implication, the imagery of St-Pierre's misericords can be seen as a bitter commentary on the profligacy of the time. Its great preoccupation with sexual license is symbolized by the presence of Mary Magdalene on one of the carvings, the only saint so singled out. She is presented in the familiar role of penitent kneeling before an open Bible; her great, unruly tresses recall not only the wildness of her early life but also her humble atoning act of drying the Savior's feet with her hair.

For medieval women the choice indicated in the misericords was between the dissolute life of the young female shown in a drunken scene with her male companion and that of marriage and woman's divinely assigned function in it, motherhood.

To castigate the men's sinful inclinations, Saumur's artists depicted no fewer than five of them in a repulsive characterization. Their faces are those of highly respectable citizens, so realistically drawn they could be parishioners. But the heads are always attached to the bodies of monsters. This virulent commentary on hypocrisy is as obvious as its corollary, that none could hide his depravity from God. But the church did not entirely abandon people to their temptations. Through the confessional, it sought to help them avoid the pit by casting a terrifying eye into their very souls.

In this grim, though marvelously carved, set one is surprised to discover a misericord with a patently buffoonish intention. It presents a man with his nose up against the front of the stall seat, in pointed juxtaposition to the lower part of the sitter's body. Photography gives us the proper meaning, however, when we study the man's face in the right-side-up position. Noting the look of terror in his eyes, one realizes that this was meant to be no laughing matter but rather one of the diabolic punishments, often seen in other church art, that sinning man could look forward to in his eternity in Hell.

84. Mary-Magdalene as Penitent (Fifteenth Century). *Saumur, Church of St-Pierre.*

85.   Dissipation (Fifteenth Century). *Saumur, Church of St-Pierre.*

86.   Mother and Infant (Fifteenth Century). *Saumur, Church of St-Pierre.*

87.   The Confessional (Fifteenth Century). *Saumur, Church of St-Pierre.*

88.   The Beast in Man (Fifteenth Century). *Saumur, Church of St-Pierre.*

89.   The Stench of Hell (Fifteenth Century). *Saumur, Church of St-Pierre.*

A State of Grace

Grown immensely wealthy in service of the kings, Robert de Balsac, military man, decided in 1482, twenty years before his death, to shore up his credits with the Eternal by setting up a splendid pious foundation in his native Auvergne.

No doubt his turbulent campaigning and intrigue had left many souvenirs to roil his conscience. He and his elder brother were, for example, accused of being intimately linked to the assassination of Count Jean V of Armagnac and his wife, an act meant to help annex that important region to France.[1]

In the foundation parchment establishing the "Chapter" of St-Chamant,[2] Balsac expressed the desire of transforming the "very numerous temporal riches" he had acquired with the Virgin's aid "into spiritual and eternal wealth." He endowed the collegiate with "a church, a cloister, houses, a library, rooms, refectories, gardens, courts, and cellars."

The site chosen by the soldier was a tranquil valley in the Auvergne highlands, where his family possessed a seigniory. He supervised much of the construction work in person; the founding document tells how he paid the masters and workmen "every day" and how he intended seeing the project through to the end.

Though nothing is known about the sculptor of the misericords, their high sophistication has occasioned the guess that he was Italian, someone possibly that Balsac had met during a three-year sojourn in that country, sent by King Louis XI to serve the Duke of Milan in "feats of war."

But sculpture of great merit was being done in many other places as well during this period: in Burgundy, for example, where the resonance of the Sluterian style was long felt, and in areas closer to St-Chamant—at Rodez, Toulouse, Moissac, even Auvergne itself.[3]

Whatever his origin, this sculptor distinguished himself by his extraordinary talent to render with unerring authenticity plain, ordinary people, laymen or clerics, in their most ignoble acts of every day. His appreciation of the charm of these banal gestures and the truth of their presentation give them a nobility that the most exalted deeds could hardly surpass. Acts on all levels of man's existence are mingled: dressing, undressing, reading, singing, dancing, playing music, embracing, together with attitudes of deep prayer and contemplation.

This great sculpture straddles the secular and the religious with perfect ease. It is not because it lacks a sense of the sacred. Quite the contrary. To every pose or gesture, no matter how humble or commonplace, it conveys the pith of beauty which lifts it to a state of grace.[4]

Other misericords from St-Chamant: Figs. 7, 50, and 53.

90. Young Woman Dressing (Fifteenth Century). *St-Cernin, Church of St-Saturnin, formerly at St-Chamant.*

91.　Woman Playing Portable Organ (Fifteenth Century). *Church of St-Chamant.*

92.   The Siren (Fifteenth Century). *Church of St-Illide, formerly at St-Chamant.*

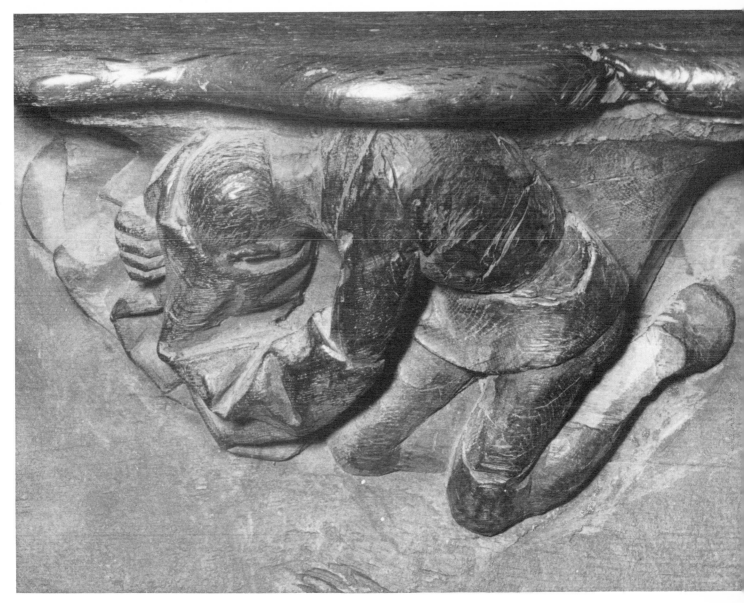

93.   Man Undressing (Fifteenth Century). *Church of St-Illide, formerly at St-Chamant.*

94. Monk Reading the Bible (Fifteenth Century). *St-Cernin, Church of St-Saturnin, formerly at St-Chamant.*

A Princess's Votive Offering

Built almost simultaneously in the first third of the sixteenth century, the two leading churches of Bourg-en-Bresse—the Collegiate of Notre-Dame and the Priory of Brou—could hardly be more different.

Notre-Dame, the city parish, the church of the bourgeoisie, is solid, unspectacular, unmarked by any feudal heraldry. The Eglise de Brou,[1] even in its present denuded state, is as splendid as a church can be.

It was built by Margaret of Austria, whose arms—along with those of Burgundy and Savoy, her other dynastic attachments—still glisten in the stained glass and on the three magnificent tombs that adorn the sanctuary.

Brou was a votive church, a fabulous commemorative mausoleum, erected by an inconsolable princess pledged to celibacy after the death of her playboy husband, Duke Philibert-the-Fair of Savoy. Built in an incredible twenty years, the spacious church is more lustrous than most cathedrals. It cost the princess at least 250,000 *florins*.[2]

Despite the blazing speed of this construction, Margaret grew impatient in the end. Heretofore on the best of terms with her architect, Louis Van Boghem, whom she sent down from Flanders in 1513, the princess suddenly, in 1530, was producing a sharp bill of complaints against him. Its main purport was a demand for even greater speed and in particular that the builder get the work started on the choir-stalls.[3] The imperious order was conjecturably obeyed that summer of 1530. But the princess was never to see the stalls, since she died a few months later.

It is not known if they were even completed by the time of the church's dedication, on March 22, 1532. If so, it would have been a phenomenal accomplishment, with seventy-five carved seats, fretted superstructure, statuary and misericords—the whole lot done in nineteen months.

There is much evidence that the carving was done at a hectic pace. One can see the chisel's chop-marks on many pieces, as though the assembler was waiting for every one and there was not time enough to buff the wood to a smoother finish.

This speed did not detract from the effectiveness of the work, however. On the contrary, it gave the sculpture an enormous surface vitality and the carved forms a throbbing immediacy akin to work in clay.

The subject matter, though without plan or continuity, fits into four general categories. One, no doubt designated by the monks of the priory, reveals them in various attitudes of prayer.

Showing a strong Flemish influence, the second subject is that of drinking. Men and even boys are shown in all attitudes of adoration of the gourd, the pitcher, or the tumbler.

The nakedness of many of them reveals a third tendency in the carving. More than half of the almost exclusively masculine set are given over to nude subjects. Sole representative of the female sex is a mother with her son—and she is thrashing his naked bottom!

The artists show still another predilection that is even more curious than nakedness. It is a kind of anal play, in which a young man or boy is always engaged with an animal.

These scenes must have been regarded as pure fantasy by the clerics or they would never have survived. But the modern eye is more disabused, seeing in this playfulness an inescapable Freudian accent.

Another misericord from the Eglise de Brou: Fig. 61.

119

95. Two Men Sharing a Wine-Flask (Sixteenth Century). *Bourg-en-Bresse, Eglise de Brou.*

96. Man Drinking, with Dog (Sixteenth Century). *Bourg-en-Bresse, Eglise de Brou.*

97. The Playful Dragon (Sixteenth Century). *Bourg-en-Bresse, Eglise de Brou.*

98. Man with Friendly Monster (Sixteenth Century). *Bourg-en-Bresse, Eglise de Brou.*

99. Mother Birching Her Son (Sixteenth Century). *Bourg-en-Bresse, Eglise de Brou.*

The Burghers' "Self"-Portraits

What a different story is that of Notre-Dame's construction![1] It got none of those thousands of *florins* that the wealthiest of princesses could keep pouring into the Eglise de Brou. Its administrator's accounts reveal an income exactly one-tenth of that royal memorial, the money coming from the people or their chaplains—the people in any case.

Bourg was at first too deeply concerned by a plague, compounded by famine, to be stirred competitively by Margaret's new project. It was a rich cleric who gave the initial impulse, in 1505, to rebuilding Notre-Dame's old choir. But the burghers did not delay long in getting involved.

When, in 1510, stalls were thought of, the citizens consented to foot the bill. Foreign artists offered their services for the job; but local pride prevailed, and it was given, at thirty *florins* a seat, to artisans "of this city and of proved skill."

Added to the contract[2] that was signed by the city's six syndics and four of the church's priests with Pierre Terrasson, master joiner, were these significant words: " . . . that these artisans make the seats according to the desire of those paying for them. . . ." The whole secret of the misericords' iconography is contained in this phrase.

Work on the church apse was proceeding when, on the night of December 1, 1514, the mass of new stone and masonry foundered, bringing down a large part of the church with it. The tragedy seems only to have spurred the effort. Even the often reluctant priests doubled their yearly contribution and the city devoted over half its annual income to the task. The structure would have been rapidly completed but for the temptation of grandeur that struck in 1515: the offer to the city of a bishopric, which had to be dearly paid for.

The change of status of Notre-Dame to an episcopal church slowed down its building pace, which suffered besides from periodic family squabbles between the priests and the parishioners. When finished, it was not without leaving some unanswered questions, particularly regarding its choir-stalls.

Did they, for example, survive the great 1514 cave-in? Or did they have to be redone? The archives say nothing about this, which inclines one to think that the originals were largely spared. Whoever finished them, whatever his background or derivation, it was a bourgeois art that was created.

One might almost say that it was done *by* the burghers. For the forty-two misericords, entirely likenesses, are actually self-portraits in the sense that their subjects posed for them exactly as they saw themselves or, in any case, as they wanted to be seen. Cantankerous or gay, serious to the point of dourness or putting on cap-and-bells to prove their goodfellowship, they are frozen into a kind of permanent caricature of their social being.

123

100. Man with Hat over His Eye (Sixteenth Century).
Bourg-en-Bresse, Collegiate Church of Notre-Dame.

101. Young Woman with Coif (Sixteenth Century). *Bourg-en-Bresse, Collegiate Church of Notre Dame.*

102. Grimacing Man (Sixteenth Century). *Bourg-en-Bresse, Church of Notre-Dame.*

103. Man with Twisted Mouth (Sixteenth Century). *Bourg-en-Bresse, Church of Notre-Dame.*

104. Man Posing as a Fool (Sixteenth Century).
Bourg-en-Bresse, Church of Notre-Dame.

A Lesson in Semantics

The fact that the churchmen of St-Claude, then an abbey, had to go to Geneva in 1449 to fetch Jean de Vitry[1] to gild their choir-stalls has in modern times been a source of reproach to civic pride. Such things were regarded differently in the Middle Ages, when the great mobility of creative artists was taken for granted. This was certainly true of the stalls and misericords, which were often produced by imported specialists.

In the nineteenth century, St-Claude scholars eagerly sought evidence that indigenous carvers might have had something to do with the creation of the cathedral's splendid stalls. Curiously, they did not think of the local makers of statuettes and paternosters in this connection, objects that were associated with a celebrated cult, that of the city's patron saint, which attracted even kings and queens on pilgrimage. People had wanted to carry a chip of St. Claude's miracle-working powers away with them, and homegrown talents developed to fashion something appropriate for the pilgrims' farthings.

It was evidently not easy for elitist-minded, nineteenth-century art historians to relate such humble practitioners to those who had sculptured the awesome mass of statuary and scrollwork that adorned the cathedral's choir. What they were searching for were "master sculptors," men with "names." With what joy did a local scholar announce, in 1884, the discovery of what could at last be regarded as "proof" of the existence of such artists.

It was a plaque from the parish of St-Romain, demolished in 1793, which had been incrusted into the wall of a house that had been built on the old church's rubble, telling of the foundation of a "mass with procession" by the "Carvers and Sculptors" of St-Claude!

The inscribed date was October 18, 1576, over a hundred years after the choir-stalls had been completed.[2] But what matter? One could argue, and cogently enough, that these artists must have had antecedents who could have participated, "at least in part," in the making of "the magnificent stalls."

Sadly, this pride of parenthood had been lacking in the eighteenth century. Around 1750, the stalls were moved way back into the rear of the apse, where they had to be mauled to fit, a large part being sliced off and relegated to the loft.

It was not for over a century, in 1869, that St-Pierre's stalls came back into honor and were returned to their present central position. But the whole lot was in a terrible state of dilapidation. "Of the thousands of pieces composing the stalls, there was not one that did not need some repair," a witness described. Robelin de Colonne, a man of the Juras, was in charge and understood his job as that of reproducing exactly the original carving.[3] That St-Claude's misericords live today is largely the result of his artisanry. That the Juras could have supplied this talent was the prize of centuries of practice in the art of carving on wood.[4]

Other misericords from St-Claude: Figs. 4, 27, and 56.

105. Portrait of Man with Elaborate Hood (Fifteenth Century).
St-Claude, Cathedral of St-Pierre.

106. Woman with Distaff (Fifteenth Century). *St-Claude, Cathedral of St-Pierre.*

107. Calvin as a Pig, in the Pulpit (Fifteenth Century). *St-Claude, Cathedral of St-Pierre.*

108. Catching the Greased Pig (Fifteenth Century). *St-Claude, Cathedral of St-Pierre.*

The Entrepreneur of Stalls

André Sulpice is associated with the making of more choir-stalls than any other known French artist. His fame rests chiefly on four great sets, contracts for three of which still exist: the Collegiate of Notre-Dame and the Chartreuse of Villefranche-de-Rouergue, the Abbey of Loc-Dieu, and Rodez Cathedral.[1] And he is credited with several others.

André Sulpice was, preeminently, an energetic entrepreneur and talent scout. His contract with Rodez specified that he was to have seven assistants at all times. But that may have been because he had gained a reputation for delay, no doubt the result of shifting men from job to job, all of which he kept going at the same time.

We first hear of him at Bourges, in 1452, when the cathedral was given a thorough overhauling, and he did the stalls. He was at Vence, near Nice, making stalls again, when he was discovered, in 1460, by the rector of the newly built Chartreuse of Villefranche, who was on his way back from Rome with the body of its merchant-founder, who had died while on pilgrimage to the papal city.

André Sulpice was occupied thereafter with his four most famous choir-stalls. But he must have found some time in-between to sire another group at Béziers, a model of which he furnished when he signed the contract with Rodez,[2] his last work. A man who had created so many sets himself would hardly have offered someone else's pattern to get an assignment.

Villefranche's municipal consuls, who were called "founders and patrons" of the Collegiate Church, were the ones who along with its canons signed the contract with Sulpice in 1473.[3] Much other evidence indicates that the burghers' role at Notre-Dame was preponderant. Thus, when the stalls were completed in 1487, the consuls, alleging that they were too massive, blocking their aspect of the high altar, demanded peremptorily that eight of the seventy seats be destroyed to clear the view.[4]

The conflict went on for four years and the consuls won out in the end. But not without violence. The city fathers on one Assumption Day locked the holy vessels and vestments away, set their maced troops at the pulpit to prevent the sermon by a famous invited preacher, and forbade the parishioners to make offerings.

When the settlement was reached, the purpose of it all became clear as the four consuls demanded and obtained seats for themselves and four other lay officials in the new choir-stalls.

It is hardly surprising that the misericords at the Collegiate Church bear a strong bourgeois imprint, as do those at Rodez. The carvings at the two churches have a strong resemblance, besides, both in the style of the figures and of the decorative detail.

The underseat work of Chartreuse and Loc-Dieu was done by other chisels, the former having included one carver with a remarkable eye for animals. Loc-Dieu's set, on the other hand, is entirely assigned to vegetation, following the antifigurative principles of the house's patron saint, St. Bernard.[5]

Where the common parentage in all sets is most evident is in the austere Gothic upper-stalls. Here André Sulpice himself placed his master's mark inescapably.

Another misericord from Villefranche Collegiate: Fig. 58.

131

109.   Woman taking Bath as Servant Pours (Fifteenth Century). *Ville-franche-de-Rouergue, Collegiate Church of Notre-Dame.*

110. Portrait of a Bourgeois Woman (Fifteenth Century).
Villefranche-de-Rouergue, Collegiate Church of Notre-Dame.

111. Double Portrait of Two Young Women (Fifteenth Century). *Rodez, Cathedral of Notre-Dame.*

112. Monk with Two Nuns Commenting the Bible (Fifteenth Century). *Rodez, Cathedral of Notre-Dame.*

113. Bird of Prey (Fifteenth Century). *Villefranche-de-Rouergue, La Chartreuse St-Sauveur.*

Created in Turmoil

It seems utterly contradictory that the stalls of Rouen Cathedral, among the most splendid of France, should in the period of their making have been the subject of an endless, abrasive controversy between the church and the artists.[1]

Minutely documented in the capitular and fabric registers, these differences are played out like a modern labor-employer conflict. In fact, the theme at issue—the speed of the work—is one that is more than familiar in our times.

The underlying source of the dispute was the fact that the agreement covering the stallwork proper—the paneling and scrollwork—called for pay by the day, which led to constant accusations of willful delay. Figure sculpture, on the other hand, was assigned by the piece and was free from such contention.

It is plain from the archives that the major problem of Philippot Viart, the stalls' master-of-works, was to find enough skilled men to keep up the pace that the churchmen demanded. At least seven missions in search of workers are on record, one of which carried the questors as far as Brussels, including stops at a dozen places on the way.[2]

The canons' obvious mistrust of Viart did not help matters. His work had had professional sanction at the start, in February 1458, when a model of a stall created by him was approved by three master-carvers under the sharp scrutiny of a group of canons, who then duly paid for a round of drinks. When, four years later, the churchmen repeated their official visit to the artists' atelier, the atmosphere must have been tense. The inspecting group was led by none other than the dean of the cathedral, and bitter accusations of procrastination had already been raised.

What makes the whole matter incredible to us is the high excellence of Viart's product. Unfortunately, there is nothing left of the upper stallwork itself, only the chairs and of course their underseat carving. But there is every reason to believe that the quality of what has vanished was up to the standard of the part that still remains.

A pertinent archival datum, in fact, mentions a contract signed by Pol Mosselmen, the chief sculptor of the upper-stall statuary. He was to receive twenty *sous* each for forty-eight big figures, the agreement says, but would also make the "carvings on six misericords," the last for a total of thirty *sous*. Five *sous* per misericord, the hire for a single day![3] Astonishing as this accomplishment may seem, it is no more so than what we learn from this same incontrovertible source about this same great artist having to sculpt an upper-stall statue in four days' time, if he were to earn at least as much as any skilled joiner did.

Pol Mosselmen, Fleming, carved sixty-six pieces of the stalls' major statuary, in addition to other sculpture. François Trubert, Frenchman, did all but one of the other twenty-two large figures. The registers identify many of them: apostles, prophets, saints, church-fathers, the seven virtues. And the lesser figurines and foliar decoration are often also carefully described, done by named artists who specialized in this work. In all, we have the names of at least thirty-two wood-carvers and sculptors who worked on the choir furniture.

137

But the man who designed Rouen's great stalls and directed their transfer from paper to wood through eleven years was not allowed to preside at their termination. Philippot Viart's relations with the chapter went into a sharp decline in mid-1466, when he was menaced with every severity if he did not press the effort.

By the following April assemblage of the stalls was begun. Still the chapter was not content and by September it was warning Viart of arrest if he did not hasten the work. In October the canons began assigning work to outside carvers—on a piecework basis! Viart's senior assistants were ordered out of the atelier and in January he himself was finally fired. But he could not tear himself away from the great project with which he had been linked for so many years. The records show him being chased again and again from the atelier. In the end, the crown's chief police officer was called in, who ordered him off under pain of a 100 *livres* fine.

Viart continued secretly to work on the stalls, nonetheless, in the house he and his family had been furnished by the chapter. The piece he was carving is identified in the archives: it was one of the stalls' end-panels, which he had somehow abstracted from the atelier. One can still see him working away at this piece when the final court order hit him: seizure of his person, that of his wife and all their belongings, the family ejected from their lodgings. Imprisonment is also mentioned. It is the last we hear of Philippot Viart.

The creative days at Rouen Cathedral of Viart's most productive assistant, Pol Mosselmen, were likewise soon ended, according to the faithful registers. In 1470, in a few terse words, a rare and signal honor nevertheless, they announce the creative Fleming's death.

Fate has been highly selective in its preservation of Rouen Cathedral's magnificent choir-stalls, of which only sixty-six misericords remain, somewhat the worse for wear but still shining in their beauty. A number of them dealt with various phases of the city's two most important industries, shoemaking and drapery, though a whole series of carvings of the latter were destroyed in one night's bombing in August, 1944. Several pieces of the shoemaker's trade still exist, on the other hand, which, together with the other underseat carvings, give an amazingly evocative picture of the life of one of France's most dynamic medieval cities.[4]

Other misericords from Rouen: Figs. 14, 16, 18, 23, 28, 32, 51.

114. Physician Examining a Man's Leg (Fifteenth Century). *Rouen, Cathedral of Notre-Dame.*

115.   The Oystermonger (Fifteenth Century). *Rouen, Cathedral of Notre-Dame.*

116. Shoemaker Fitting a Client for a Pair of Boots (Fifteenth Century). *Rouen, Cathedral of Notre-Dame.*

117. The Log-Splitter (Fifteenth Century). *Rouen, Cathedral of Notre-Dame.*

118. The Stone-Mason (Fifteenth Century). *Rouen, Cathedral of Notre-Dame.*

Carvings from a Phantom Chapel

Elegant though it is, the choir-stall ensemble of St-Denis, near Paris, lacks much of the original set created for the Château de Gaillon. Important parts can be found in half a dozen private collections and museums, notably at the Cluny Museum.

The set suffered far more after than during the Revolution, when Gaillon Château itself was victimized. Acquired by the State in 1801, it soon began its century of wanderings from museum to museum, now cut up by official "restorers," now packed away in warehouses, whole sections pilfered, sold.[1]

A major interest of Gaillon's stalls resides in their transitional style. Done from 1508 to 1518, they are a priceless model of the Italian Renaissance making its early imprint on French plastic art.

Curiously, the stalls' artists, a number of whom are cited in the remarkable *Comptes* of the Château's construction,[2] were all apparently French themselves. The master-of-works was a carver of Rouen, Colin Castille, called "sculptor of antiquity."[3]

But a number of Italian artists also worked at the Château, from whom the Frenchmen are considered to have acquired their Renaissance briefings. Thus, in the Chapel for which the stalls were created, Andrea Solario, pupil of Leonardo, did a fresco of Cardinal Georges d'Amboise, builder of Gaillon, and his numerous brothers, no fewer than four of whom were bishops.

Georges d'Amboise was one of the most sumptuous ecclesiastics of his time. Archbishop of Rouen, for whose prelates he built this superb "house of *plaisance*," then Cardinal and Papal Legate, he was Louis XII's candidate for the papacy in 1503 but was tricked out of the post by the puissant Giuliano de la Rovere (Julius II). His political role was as prodigious as his churchly one and a great part of his royal guerdon went toward creating Gaillon: expenditures of 153,600 *livres* being listed in the *Comptes* for half of its building years.

The Renaissance style is richly illustrated in the part of the stalls still extant at St-Denis. There is not a square centimeter that has not been worked on: statues, armrests, terminal pieces, paneling in low relief and in colored wooden marquetry. Unfortunately, the misericords themselves have been badly hacked. But even so one recognizes in them a unique style, the actors being presented as though on a proscenium while the entire underseat area around them is enlivened by a rich décor resembling a stage set. The ensemble is unmatched in France.

A few of the carvings have been relatively spared. One of the finest shows a group of musicians giving a recital: an organist, varied woodwind and string instrumentalists and—prize of them all—a female cantatrice with a music scroll in her hands.

St-Denis's stalls contain one remnant of another once important set: the abbot's throne from St-Lucien-de-Beauvais.[4] Many other misericords from this once famous abbey, now a skeleton, can be seen at the Cluny Museum.[5]

Other misericords from St-Lucien-de-Beauvais, now at the Cluny Museum: Figs. 36, 52, and 57.

119. The Musical Recital (Sixteenth Century).
Basilica of St-Denis, formerly at the Chapel of the
Château de Gaillon.

120. The Conversion of St. Eustace (Sixteenth Century). *Basilica of St-Denis, formerly at the Chapel of the Château de Gaillon.*

121. Dance of the Putti (Sixteenth Century). *Basilica of St-Denis, formerly at the Chapel of the Château de Gaillon.*

122. Dance of the Putti, Seen in Its Choir-Seat Ensemble (Sixteenth Century). *Basilica of St-Denis, formerly at the Chapel of the Château de Gaillon.*

The "Grammar of Classicism"

There are a small number of stall sets of the sixteenth century, particularly in south and southwest France, which differentiate themselves sharply from the style and spirit of the great majority, whose basic characteristic assimilates them to Gothic art.

It is not so much a matter of sophistication as of cosmology. French misericords of the period remain fundamentally Christian. Those of Auch and St-Bertrand-de-Comminges[1] and a few other churches take much of their inspiration from pagan antiquity. Theirs is, in other words, art of the early French Renaissance, their main source of influence, Italy. That the churches of Auch and St-Bertrand actually called on artists from that country to create their stalls remains only conjectural, however.

Nevertheless, circumstantial evidence of such participation is rather strong, particularly at the Cathedral of Sainte-Marie of Auch. The three archbishop-cardinals there, during whose terms the vastest and most elaborate stalls of France were erected, were all men of broad Italian background.

François de Clermont-Lodève, who started the work going around 1515, soon after taking his post, was fresh out of Italy, where he had served as Louis XII's ambassador for a number of years. His nephew and successor, François-Jacques de Tournon, also was ambassador to Rome. Last of the trio was an Italian himself, Ippolito d'Este, son of Lucrezia Borgia and Alphonse I of Ferrara. Too exalted a personage to serve in a transalpine archbishopric, he had his place filled by a vicar, Pietro di Ghinucci, also an Italian.[2]

St-Bertrand's stalls did not have the serried importance of Auch's patronage. But its donor, Bishop Jean de Mauléon, did come from a noble family that had pretensions to a Roman origin of high estate, besides. He, too, knew Italy, whose influence is especially noticeable in the medallion portraits and in the rich marquetry work of the great choir enclosure.

As for St-Bertrand's misericords, though Renaissance in spirit, they are far less ornate than those of Auch, which swarm with antique gods and goddesses, harpies and putti and satyrs. There is a quiet dignity about St-Bertrand's underseat carvings, and one can still find an Adam and Eve and a Temptation of Christ on the central ramps, solemnly dominating the stalls.

Into the seventeenth century, the antique world continued to increase its influence over misericord carving. At Moissac, Toulouse, Moutier-d'Ahun, and other places the "grammar of classicism" took over the underseat space. But the quality was not enhanced. Though the decorative art of the stallwork at times attained an extraordinary baroque exuberance, as at Moutier, the misericords themselves exhibited an overall declining inventive power.

Other misericords from Auch and St-Bertrand: Figs. 1, 9, and 55.

123. Infant Christ with Angels Bearing the
Flagella (Sixteenth Century). *Auch, Cathedral of
Ste-Marie.*

124. Satire of Calvinists Commenting the
Bible (Sixteenth Century). *Auch, Cathedral of
Ste-Marie.*

125. Two Young Fauns in Decorative Setting (Sixteenth Century). *Auch, Cathedral of Ste-Marie.*

126. Hercules and Antaeus (Sixteenth Century). *Auch, Cathedral of Ste-Marie.*

127. A Sibyl (Sixteenth Century). *St-Bertrand-de-Comminges, Church of Notre-Dame.*

128. Portrait of a Nobleman (Sixteenth Century). *St-Bertrand-de-Comminges, Church of Notre-Dame.*

129. Old Satyr and Young Nymph (Sixteenth Century). *St-Bertrand-de-Comminges, Church of Notre-Dame.*

130.   Sagittarius (Sixteenth Century). *St-Bertrand-de-Comminges, Notre-Dame.*

A Conscientious Prelate's Message

There is no iconographic program or other documentary source to account for the unique evangelical content of Auxerre's misericords. It is interesting, at least, that we are informed about the person who was responsible for their creation.[1] However, it is not certain that the position of this individual, Bishop Jacques Amyot, who held St-Etienne's cathedra from 1571 to 1593, satisfactorily explains their New Testament imagery. He was not the only prelate who paid for his church's choir-stalls, after all.

Shortly before Jacques Amyot had taken office, the iconoclastic Huguenots had worked the church over with their arquebuses, leaving much of its art beyond recognition. The new prelate launched immediately and zealously into the restoration, beginning with the choir furniture. The stalls were rebuilt by 1574.

By all accounts, the bishop was a most conscientious churchman. Son of a modest haberdasher of Melun, his extraordinary gift for Latin and Greek made a scholastic vocation automatic. University professor, translator of Plutarch, preceptor of royal princes, his career moved steadily up the hierarchic ladder. As he himself profiled his life's story, Jacques Amyot was filled with trepidation when he took over the Auxerre prelacy at fifty-eight, realizing that his literary background, which had limited his reading to "profane authors," had left him ill-adapted for an apostolic calling.

Setting himself assiduously to the task of correcting his shortcoming, he concentrated on the study of holy scripture. Rising every morning at five, he reports, he spent most of his day in reading or discussing fine points of exegetics with well-known theologians whom he invited to Auxerre.

He deferred out of diffidence, for as long as possible, taking the pulpit, getting chevroned substitutes to fill his place. When he finally mustered the courage to give his first sermon, he delivered it while seated—from the handsome rostrum he had had built to replace the one the Huguenots had destroyed.

There are over forty recognizable subjects of New Testament origin among Auxerre's misericords and a number of others that have had a similar imagery but that were too mutilated during the Revolution to be firmly identifiable today. Such a program could only have been designed by a cleric. Was it Jacques Amyot?

Actually, it hardly matters whether it was that concerned man or not since, in any case, it must have been done with his knowledge and consent. The question is why the almost universal ban against the use of New Testament themes in the underseat carving, which had always been observed so rigidly, was breached in this case.

It is possible that the answer lies in a change of habit by the canons. No longer bound by ascetic practices at that late date, they could have abandoned use of the underseat ledges and frankly relaxed during offices in the broad regular seats. These, then, would be kept lifted when not in use, for appreciation of their ornamentation.

Such an accounting is lacking in the only other nearly exclusive set of New Testament subjects that we know of in France: the one at the charming pilgrimage church of St-Sulpice-de-Favières, which was done much earlier, moreover.[2]

Another misericord from Auxerre: Fig. 29.

131. Christ and the Adulteress (Sixteenth Century). *Aux-erre, Cathedral of St-Etienne.*

132. The Parable of the Sower (Sixteenth Century). *Auxerre, Cathedral of St-Etienne.*

133.   Christ Saving Peter from the Waters (Sixteenth Century).
Auxerre, Cathedral of St-Etienne.

134. The Harrowing of Hell (Sixteenth Century). *Auxerre, Cathedral of St-Etienne.*

135. Joseph Teaching Carpentry to the Young Jesus (Fifteenth Century). *Church of St-Sulpice-de-Favières.*

136. Christ Tempted by Satan (Fifteenth Century). *Church of St-Sulpice-de-Favieres.*

A Proud City's Pageant Play

France's most famous choir-stalls, those of Notre-Dame-d'Amiens, have left scant primary data about the circumstances of their creation. What we know comes to us by second hand since the original documents have disappeared and those who saw them long ago were infuriatingly slipshod in their recordings.[1]

We have but eight names of artists who worked on the carving, four of them only summarily cited. Two men, Ernoul Boulin and Alexandre Huet,[2] shared the overall responsibility. Each was given charge of half the set, right and left, as though in a friendly emulative contest. And friends they were, living in the same street in neighboring houses.

Two other important artists included Antoine Avernier,[3] "figure-carver," who was hired to do seventy-two historiated reliefs, probably mostly misericords, and Jehan Trupin, who appeared on the lists only three years before the set was finished, in 1519, but has the most famous name of all.

Authors have sought to downgrade Trupin's contribution, his reported pay being only three *sous* a day, the hire of an ordinary workman. But an error is obvious since Trupin's name is the only one of an artist inscribed on the stalls. In fact it appears two times on them, with decorative flourish (see Fig. 5).

Little is known, also, of the contributors to the stalls' cost, which amounted to nearly 9,500 *livres*. Of this sum, only one-seventh can be definitely accounted for, all of it given by churchmen. If other patrons were known, however, it is almost certain that wealthy burghers would be among them. For Amiens's citizens, who governed their city from early in the twelfth century, were always intensely active in the life of its cathedral and repeatedly made significant contributions to its building and decoration.[4] Bourgeois patronage of the stalls seems all the more likely in light of the popular style of their art and notably of the misericords.

Amiens's one hundred ten underseat carvings are given over exclusively to Old Testament subjects, eighty-eight of which are devoted to three patriarchs, Jacob, Joseph,[5] and Moses, whose stories lend themselves eminently to a social or even familial interpretation.

These characterizations are often imbued with a great warmth, as exemplified by such scenes as the infant Moses's choice of his mother as his wet nurse, Rebecca's sorrow on leaving home, Jacob's shock when told of his mother's plan to deceive his father Isaac, or Joseph's emotion at meeting his brother Benjamin. No doubt Amiens's burghers identified more intimately with such human episodes than with the momentous doctrinal significance of the described events as seen in the Rebecca-and-Jacob story, for example.

In addition to the misericords' dramatic pageantry, all linked by a serpentine of Old Testament interludes carved on the ramps of the stalls' terminal panels, there is an immense richness of popular subjects in the armrests and upper-stall decoration, which swarms with a great forest of botanical and zoological life. The panels themselves are animated by some forty bas-reliefs of New Testament scenes.

Only large statues of saints and prophets, such as so frequently appear in other choirs, are missing. Did the Amiens planners feel that their stalls were already too loaded down with sculpture? Such a thought did not seem otherwise to influence the makers of these stalls, where 3,650 figures have been counted.

It seems likely that something entirely different was involved—a kind of reluctance to introduce oversize figures of any kind in this great human panoply. This could have been due to an instinct of democratic estheticism, which would have been in keeping, moreover, with the political reality of this proud, self-governing city.

137. Matchmaker Eliezer Brings Presents from Isaac to Rebecca (Sixteenth Century). *Amiens, Cathedral of Notre-Dame.*

138. Rebecca's Sorrow as She Leaves Home with Eliezer (Sixteenth Century). *Amiens, Cathedral of Notre-Dame.*

139. Rebecca Pregnant with Her First Child (Sixteenth Century). *Amiens, Cathedral of Notre-Dame.*

140. Esau Sells His Birthright to Jacob for a Plate of Lentils (Sixteenth Century). *Amiens, Cathedral of Notre-Dame.*

141. Rebecca Prepares to Disguise Jacob with Goatskins (Sixteenth Century).
Amiens, Cathedral of Notre-Dame.

142. The Blind Isaac Blessing Jacob Disguised as Esau (Sixteenth Century).
Amiens, Cathedral of Notre-Dame.

143. Jacob's Dream of the Ladder and God's Promise to Him (Sixteenth Century). *Amiens, Cathedral of Notre-Dame.*

144. Jacob Wrestles with the Angel Until He Blesses Him, Naming Him Israel (Sixteenth Century). *Amiens, Cathedral of Notre-Dame.*

Apotheosis of the Object

What is most remarkable about the misericords of St-Jean-de-Maurienne is the large number of individual objects depicted, each shown by and for itself. There are over two dozen of them among the carvings, more than enough to indicate some special design or program.

Some have suggested that they are donor symbols of guilds that were once active at St-Jean. But scholars[1] have found no evidence of such guilds, having identified merely three pious confraternities with professional attachments in that city. There are, besides, certain of the carved objects that it would be difficult to identify with any trade. Such are the homely turnip, the mountain rose, the seven-pointed star.

The three dice shown in a fateful cast, on the other hand, could very well have spoken for a dice-makers' organization if one had existed at St-Jean. For dice-makers did have guilds in the Middle Ages, whose "signature"—two gamblers—can be seen on a high stained-glass lancet over Chartres Cathedral's choir, for example.

It is known that St-Jean had a kind of corporative council, made up of representatives of the clergy, the nobility, and the bourgeoisie. This group was assembled by announcement at mass, by town criers, and by church bells. Presided over by the bishop's vicar, its sessions were in all likelihood held in the cathedral choir.

Whatever else they probably do not represent, the twenty-eight carved objects among St-Jean's eighty-one misericords are a roll call of the city's productive life: knives, eye-glasses, gloves, belts, pouches, money-bags, bellows, inkwells, leather cases, pitchers, pails, brooms, mallets, wine-casks, rings, carved shells, architects' instruments. . . .

That the artist who conceived and executed this admirable gallery should have had so high a regard for the industry of St-Jean's inhabitants is amazing enough for that early period. It is doubly so that he should have presented it in this striking way—each article posed as though for its portrait, each with its own "personality" conveyed with a depth and sharpness that could typify the work of the finest still-life artist.

They seem to be exposed to us as though under a magnifying glass. But we do not mean size or sharper detail, but rather something much more meaningful. Were we not reluctant to be considered mystical, we might say that they all seem inhabited by a soul. Together, they constitute a kind of Glorification of the Object.

Another misericord from St-Jean-de-Maurienne: Fig. 6.

145. The Dice (Fifteenth Century). *St-Jean-de-Maurienne,
Cathedral of St-Jean-Baptiste.*

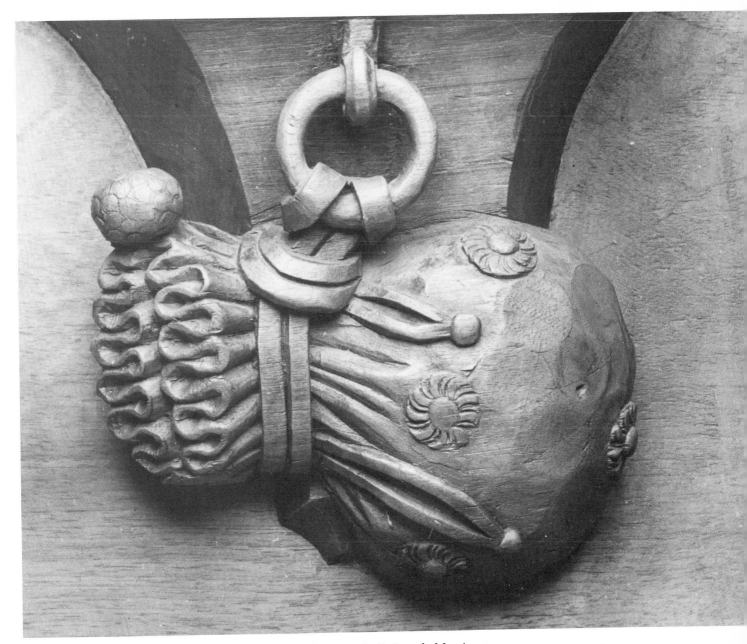

146. The Full Purse (Fifteenth Century). *St-Jean-de-Maurienne,*
Cathedral of St-Jean-Baptiste.

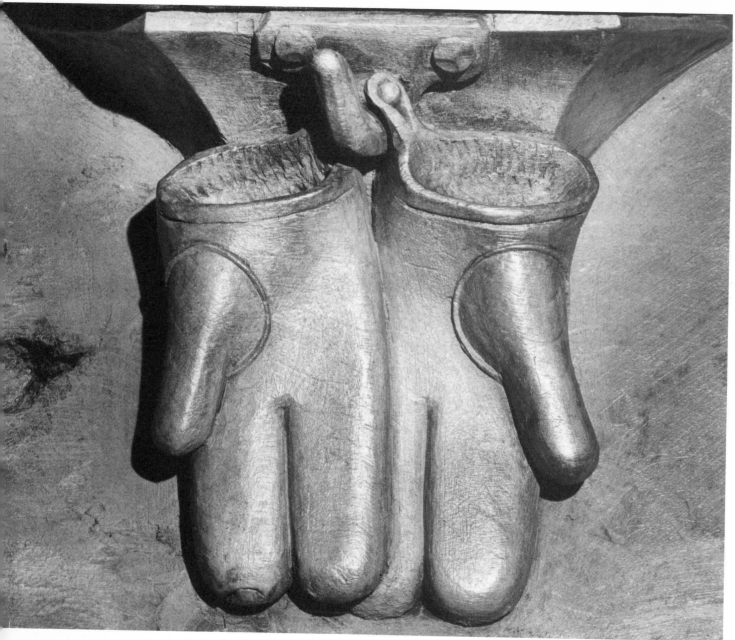

147. A Pair of Gloves (Fifteenth Century). *St-Jean-de-Maurienne, Cathedral of St-Jean-Baptiste.*

148. Two Keys (Fifteenth Century). *St-Jean-de-Maurienne, Cathedral of St-Jean-Baptiste.*

149. The Turnip (Fifteenth Century). *St-Jean-de-Maurienne, Cathedral of St-Jean-Baptiste.*

Misericords of Other Countries

Great Britain

Among the other countries with important collections of misericords, Great Britain, with thirty-five hundred catalogued carvings, merits primary consideration.

The most striking aspect of these British misericords is their precocity, a number of the finest sets being assigned by their scholars to the fourteenth century. Included are the carvings of Winchester (c. 1305), Chichester (c. 1330), Ely (1338), Gloucester (1345), Lincoln (1370), and many others.[1]

There is nothing in France of the contemporary period to compare with the sophistication of the English work. Of over five hundred fourteenth-century French misericords collated in our survey, all but a handful are of elementary design. One is tempted to conjecture that the Hundred Years' War slowed down French stall production and hence development.

Actually, the extant early misericord carving of no other country comes up to the English standard, not even the highly reputed Belgian work, whose leading remaining sets are dated from around 1430 to 1550. England's prematurity is difficult to account for and clearly needs comparative study.

Whatever the explanation of this apparent discrepancy, the individuality of English misericords is patent. This is as true of the style of the sculpture as it is of the arrangement of its parts or the imagery. The subject matter in particular often strikes a lively, indigenous note, as in the punishment of the dishonest alewife (Ludlow), the woman serving a calf's head for her husband's dinner (St. David's Cathedral), a housewife scaring off a fox with a stick (Ely), a man being devoured by wolves (Boston), and numerous others.

While the mermaid, symbolizing sexual seduction, can be found in the misericords of all countries, the one at the port town of Boston has a charming topicality, the siren being shown practicing her wiles on two local sailors. Was this meant as a solacing thought to wives whose seafaring husbands had disappeared: that they might still free themselves from the wanton's clutches and return?

A local artist tended if anything to enhance the uniqueness of his effort. A striking example can be seen at the charming country church of Ripple, in Worcestershire, where the Labors of the Months were taken straight from life: hedging and ditching, gathering corn for malting, bird-scaring, collecting dead branches for fuel.

In the overall, British misericord themes are as richly varied as those of any other country: animals, games, proverbs, religious topics, work, and domestic scenes. Feudal literary references and fabliaux seem to be more common than in France, perhaps because of the earlier dating of the English carving.

The most distinguishing stylistic feature of British misericords undoubtedly is the possession of wing carvings, the so-called supporters, on both sides of the central sculpture. Appearing first as scrolled extensions, like a flourish to a signature, they swiftly evolved in iconographic expression, often fitting into the major theme. It is astonishing that this brilliant English initiative was rarely imitated in other countries. At

171

Albi Cathedral, about one-third of the misericords have wing carvings but they lack the English diversity. In a few other places, we have seen French misericords with added features at the sides. But they remained isolated exceptions.

That so much English underseat carving should have survived Protestant iconoclasm was no doubt due in large measure to its prevailingly secular subject matter. Since a huge proportion of the country's other medieval art treasures was destroyed, this part that has been spared seems all the more precious.

One must say that the English fully appreciate their possession. In other countries, in France particularly, the misericords are all but ignored, neglected, some of the finest of them almost appearing to disintegrate before one's eyes. It is very much different in England, where the perseverant pursuit of the subject by scholars is unmatched elsewhere. A number of churches have excellent brochures devoted to their misericords. Seats are kept lifted in the open chancel, the carvings glowingly exposed.

Belgium

Extravagant claims about the role of Flemish artists in the creation of stalls and misericords in other countries have raised many nationalistic hackles. The art historian Francis Bond was impelled to declare in defense of his country's work that the "great majority" of its stalls were as "thoroughly English as the oak of which they are built."[2]

The contention was exacerbated by the Belgian author, Louis Maeterlinck,[3] whose chauvinistic pretensions have tended to obscure the unquestionable influence that Flemish sculptors did have on the work of other countries.

In England itself, medieval officials are seen trying to attract Flanders artisans by vaunting their country's good beer, soft beds, and pretty girls. A Scottish merchant, donor of the stalls of Melrose Abbey, makes handsome offers to a master carver from Bruges. Flemish participation on Windsor, Westminster, and other sets is acknowledged by British authors.

In Germany and most particularly in Spain, the contribution of men from Flanders has been marked. As for France, though archives show that the great majority of its stall-carvers were native, the presence of Flemings has been established in some places. In others, style and subject matter reflect their imprint.

We cannot ignore either the attraction that artists of other countries felt toward Flemish work or the reasons for its appeal. It was the popular nature of much of this art that must have fascinated the sculptors, whose freedom of thematic choice when working with misericords facilitated imitation.

In Flanders, the popular spirit was fostered by the important role that burghers played in art patronage. This was in keeping with their social and political prominence which for lengthy periods rose to actual hegemony in great drapery and trading centers like Bruges and Ghent.

Belgian underseat carving is of very high quality. This is especially true of the seven great sets that still remain at Diest, Aarschot, Hoogstraten, Walcourt, St-Sauveur of Bruges, and the two churches of St-Pierre and Ste-Gertrude at Louvain.[4]

There is a tendency to exaggerate the rowdyish element in Flemish misericords. This impression stems in fact from a small minority of the carvings. At Walcourt, what appears to be sexual lewdness may actually be only a curious antimasculine prejudice. In one piece a woman has roped a man by the penis, in another she sprinkles it with water, while in a third, two naked couples fight a mock combat, the women mounted on the men who are extended on all fours. And this strange bias is not confined to the misericords, for a terminal relief presents the serpent of the Temptation as a bearded man!

Still the great majority of the church's forty misericords are innocent of suggestive themes and include a number of scriptural pieces, work scenes, and other subjects. Indeed, Flemish subject matter is as varied as that of any other country. Religious topics in particular are common, especially at Louvain's Ste-Gertrude, where they are almost an exclusive.

The frequent references to drinking and drunkenness in Belgian misericords usually have a homiletic accent. The drunkard riding a pig at Hoogstraten symbolizes the degenerative effect of alcohol on man, whereas the man in a sodden torpor outside his house at cock-crow who is refused entrance by his wife depicts the family problems that drink engenders.

Numerous subjects delineate proverbs, to which a subtle ingredient may be added to give increased zest to the allusion. This is the case with two further misericords at Hoogstraten which illustrate the joint sayings: "Little noise, much wool" and "Much noise, little wool."

The sculptor has seized the occasion to deliver a bit of radical social commentary. The man shearing the plump sheep of its curly nap is a richly garbed burgher engaged in a paradoxical task while the poor peasant with his culottes and wooden clogs has only a squealing pig to work on![5]

Germany

A great number of Germany's medieval stalls have been deprived of their misericords.[6] The process has been going on for a long time. When, for example, the stalls were destroyed in the Second World War at Cologne's St. Gereon church, there were no interesting misericords left to be obliterated.

The surviving stalls themselves may still have magnificent sculpture, as at Memmingen and Berchtesgaden (formerly Weingarten). But the underseat carvings at both are purely formal. In Protestant areas, misericords tended to disappear when their purpose ended with the abolition of the incessant offices of the clerical community. Nevertheless, the new religion often maintained the beautiful old choir furniture. But the stalls' occupants were now mostly laymen: wealthy burghers, the mayor and the city council, guild leaders.

German authors admit the derivative nature of many of their misericords.[7] In contrast is the striking originality of much of the country's upperstall carving, of which they are justifiably proud. This can be seen in a memorable set at Ulm Cathedral where the great innovator Jörg Syrlin was master-of-works. The most notable feature of this sculpture is a splendid series of busts depicting ancient sibyls and philosophers who were supposed to typify the pre-Christian "longing" for salvation. While reflecting the new humanist spirit of the time, they assumed the actual features of rich patricians of the important Danube city.[8]

But Ulm also has misericords that are consistent with its stall-work. And there are other churches in Germany where high-grade underseat carving subsists. In the Eastern Sector, fine sets can be found at Stendal and Magdeburg, for example. In the northwest, the beautiful misericords of Cologne Cathedral are ascribed to the fourteenth century. They illustrate what German authors have said about foreign influence, since some of the underseat carvings have a strong affinity to Belgian work whereas the style of others has obviously been inspired by Reims Cathedral's monumental sculpture.

173

Switzerland

Interesting sets of misericords in Switzerland are found in only a fraction of the remaining choir-stalls. Paul L. Ganz, in a comprehensive work, lists about a dozen collections of underseat carvings with varied, figured subjects out of close to two hundred extant stall-groups.[9]

Significantly, not one of these misericord sets was created later than the early sixteenth century. This strongly implies the impact of the Reformation, and while Ganz declares that stalls were "seldom destroyed" by the Protestants (unless the church unit itself was wiped out), the new religionists did not, in any case, themselves build stalls with noteworthy misericords. The finest underseat sculpture in Switzerland was done in the fifteenth and sixteenth centuries. There is some interesting earlier work, as at Magdenau and Magerau, but it is very scarce.

Another contemporary author, Robert Berton, has demonstrated a close concordance in the style of thirteen outstanding "Gothic stalls" still remaining in Switzerland and in the surrounding area.[10] They were carved from 1449 to 1526. Eight of these stalls are located in Switzerland itself, three of which still have their fascinating misericords: Lausanne Cathedral and the churches of Moudon and Estavayer-le-Lac.

Other stalls of the important "Gothic" group still possessing sets of misericords are outside of present-day Switzerland: two at Aosta, Italy (the Cathedral and the Collegiate Church), and three in French churches, at Evian-les-Bains, St-Claude, and St-Jean-de-Maurienne.

In the fifteenth century, Basel and the area roundabout were highly productive in stall-art, of which little remains today. Some remnants of a ravishing set of misericords at Basel Cathedral, carved around 1430, are now housed at the Stadtmuseum while a larger part of both stalls and misericords was recarved and reassembled at the church itself.

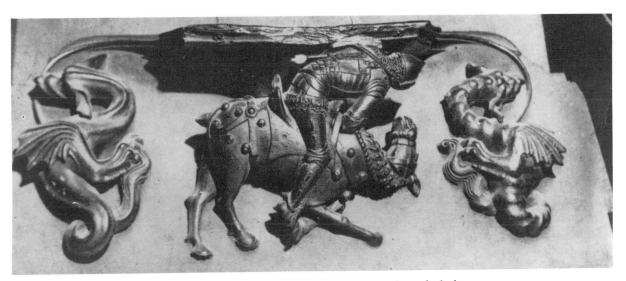

150. Wounded Knight Falling from His Horse (Fourteenth Century). *Lincoln Cathedral.*

151. Fiddler and Dancer (Fourteenth Century). *Chichester Cathedral.*

175

152.   Woodcarver at Work. Supporters: His Initials (Fifteenth Century). *London, Victoria and Albert Museum.*

153.   Samson Carrying Off the Gates of Gaza (Fifteenth Century). *Ripon Minster.*

154. The Ball-Players (Fourteenth Century). *Gloucester Cathedral.*

155. Proverb: "He Who Sups with the Devil Needs a Long Spoon" (Fifteenth Century). *Windsor Castle, St. George's Chapel.*

156. The Drowsing Man (Fifteenth Century). *Diest, Church of St-Sulpice.*

157. The Apple Thief (Fifteenth Century). *Diest, Church of St-Sulpice.*

158. Peasant De-lousing His Dog (Sixteenth Century).
Hoogstraten, Church of Ste-Catherine.

159. The Winner Gets the Man (Sixteenth Century).
Hoogstraten, Church of Ste-Catherine.

160. Fable of the Crane Who Invites the Fox to Dinner (Fifteenth Century). *Aarschot, Church of Notre-Dame.*

161. Mother Teaching Child to Ride a Tricycle (Fifteenth Century). *Bruges, Church of St-Sauveur.*

162. Proverb: "Little Noise, Much Wool" (Sixteenth Century).
Hoogstraten, Church of Ste-Catherine.

163. The Beggar (Fifteenth
Century). *Ulm Cathedral.*

164. The Lovers (Fourteenth Century). *Cologne Cathedral.*

165. Dancing Woman (Fifteenth Century?). *Cologne Cathedral.*

166. The Vice of Unchastity (Fifteenth Century).
Stendal Cathedral, East Germany.

167. Lovers' May-Bath (Fifteenth Century). *Basel, Stadt-und-Münster Museum.*

169. The Thief (Fifteenth-Sixteenth Century). *Aosta (Italy), Collegiate Church of St-Pierre and St-Ours.*

Notes

PREFACE

1. The Ministry of Culture's *Monuments Historiques* registry lists stalls but not misericords. Since we had discovered by other means that a number of these stalls possessed underseat carvings too, it was an open question how many others had them. The three-hundred-odd sets of old stalls listed by the *Monuments* (total up to 1972) were the chief basis of the mailed survey that we undertook to resolve this question.

2. Various reasons have been offered for the scarcity of misericords in Italy: shortage of wood, lack of early experience in wood-carving, in which northern countries had a strong tradition, late retention of stone seats because of the more clement weather. We checked the photographic files of the Kunsthistorisches Institut at Florence, which contain a considerable number of handsome stalls but few misericords. Visits to the churches of several cities substantiated this scarcity.

3. Louis Maeterlinck did a thorough study of Belgium's misericords in 1910 (*Le genre satirique: sculpture flamande et wallonne*). Francis Bond's pioneer work on English wood-carving appeared that same year (*Wood-carving in English Churches: I. Misericords; II. Stalls*). A complete catalogue of British misericords was published by G. L. Remnant in 1969 (*A Catalogue of Misericords in Great Britain*) with an iconographic essay by Mary D. Anderson.

THE MISERICORD AS OBJECT OF UTILITY AND ART

1. References to the early development of the sitting indulgence are found in various sources. Those quoted here are from Du Cange's *Glossarium,* IV, 1845, and Fritz Neugass, *Mittelalterliches Chorgestühl in Deutschland,* 1927.

2. The *scabella sedibus inhaerentia* citation is quoted in G. Bonnenfant, *Notre-Dame d'Evreux,* 1939.

3. Our own survey revealed 2 churches with thir-teenth-century misericords—Poitiers Cathedral and Notre-Dame-de-la-Roche—and 14 with carvings of the fourteenth century. The fifteenth century had 94; sixteenth, 116; seventeenth, 121; eighteenth, 126. It must be said, however, that after the sixteenth century there is a sharp decline in the quality and overall interest of the misericords.

4. The *constabulari* are referred to as being in charge of assigning choir-stalls in a Latin register at the departmental archives of Rouen, G. 2087 (1361 or 1365), which gives the order in which the canons at Séez Cathedral were to be seated.

5. In actual figures, we collated 7,639 misericords in our survey, as of November 1973, but this figure has been augmented since. Regarding scriptural occurrences that we found, 192 were from the Old Testament (110 from Amiens) and 69 from the New Testament (41 from Auxerre).

6. The Laurent Isbré quotation is from the Archives Départementales de la Seine-Maritime (Rouen), G. 2492 (1458).

7. The claim that carvers misread source material is by Mary Anderson in her essay introducing the Remnant *Catalogue.*

8. Provenances of the hand-me-down sets, for which our own survey has listed sixty-six churches, include some of the most famous of French medieval religious houses: Clairvaux, Fontevrault, Chaalis, St-Victor, Bec, St-Lucien-prés-Beauvais, Chezal-Benoît. . . .

9. The departments of the Moselle, Nord, Pas-de-Calais, and Haute-Marne added no single set of even mediocre interest to our listing.

10. Supporting references for the identification of sculptors and other cognate data will be found in the studies devoted to individual churches in the second part of the book. Space is not available even there for the full listing of this material, which will be recorded in a completely annotated article we are preparing for publication.

11. The denigrating remark about misericord carvers is again from Mary Anderson's essay.

12. The Pol Mosselmen source will be found in the Rouen Cathedral article in the second part of the book.

13. The Troyes reference is from the Archives Départementales de l'Aube, G. 1592, quoted by Piétresson de Saint-Aubin, in the *Société d'Emulation d'Abbeville*, 1922/24, p. 401, n. 1.

14. The Amiens and Saumur sources will be found in the articles devoted to these churches. The *livre*, though varying greatly according to country and even province as well as time, had an equivalent value of at least one hundred dollars in today's money, around 1500.

ICONOGRAPHIC PATTERNS

The Daughters of Eve

1. Naming the Caen female "Venus" may not be hyperbolic since this church's collection of misericords includes a whole series of antique divinities done in the style of a popular picture-book mythology.

The Carnival Spirit

2. Regarding the Fools' Bishop, in the world of chess this would be a tautology since a "bishop" in French is a "*fou*," that is, a fool.

Music and Dancing

3. It is worth noting that another piece in the St-Cernin (St-Chamant) set may add authenticity to our interpretation of the dancing man as King David. It is that of Samson and the lion: his apparel is similar to that of David.

The World of Religion

4. We collated a total of 159 nonscriptural religious subjects in 64 churches.

5. Illustrations of misericords castigating Calvin will be found under Auch and St-Claude Cathedrals.

THE OUTSTANDING FRENCH COLLECTIONS

Wine-Merchants and Apothecaries

1. In addition to St-Victor, the following Parisian churches are known to have had stalls: Dominicans; Franciscans; Bernardines; Les Grands-Carmes; Les Mathurins; St-Germain-des-Prés; Notre-Dame-des-Victoires; Monastère-de-la-Merci; St-Jacques-aux-Pèlerins; Chapel of Collège de Cluny; and Notre-Dame, whose fourteenth-century stalls were identified from a seventeenth-century drawing of Israel Silvestre by Marcel Aubert in *L'Architecture*, 1926. Those at present in the cathedral are of the eighteenth century.

2. Louis Regnier, a nineteenth-century archivist, spent years tracking down the "lost" St-Victor stalls. See especially his article in the *Bull. Archeol. du Comité des Travaux Historiques et Scientifiques*, 1922.

3. The claim about the Port-Royal provenance is based on the flimsy circumstance that there is a set of crescents on one misericord at St-Gervais. This emblem was on the arms of Henri II, who was supposed to have endowed Port-Royal's stalls. But it also belonged to the blazon of other personages.

4. The best overall sources for St-Gervais's misericords are the two books by Louis Brochard, who was its curé for many years: *St-Gervais*, 1938, and *St-Gervais, histoire et paroisse*, 1950.

The Defiant Churchmen

1. Source of du Juigné's decree: *Inventaire-Sommaire des Archives de Seine-et-Marne*, II, 1864, G. 187.

2. The French original of the proverb, "Small rain calms big wind," is "Petite pluie abat grand vent," a pun on the words "van" (wicker-basket) and "vent" (wind).

3. Details regarding the creation of the stalls are from the above-cited source, *Inventaire-Sommaire*, G. 159.

4. Identification of the person on the anvil as a woman may raise a question, but in the similar subject at Auch Cathedral there is no doubt about her sex.

The Hunt of the Artichoke-Gobbler

1. The contract and other matters regarding St-Tugdual's stalls were discovered in a parchment of twenty folios by Anatole Barthélemy, who published them in his *Mélanges historiques et archéologiques sur la Bretagne*, I, 1856.

2. The information about the iron-carrying boats was discovered in the documents of a confraternity to which boat-owners belonged, paying to it six deniers for every ton-cask they handled. Arthur de la Broderie, in his *Histoire municipale de la ville de Tréguier: Documents iné-*

dits du 16e et du 17e siècle, 1894, where these documents were first published, suggests that there were other ships using the city's port whose masters did not belong to this confraternity.

3. The misericord artichoke, which has one or two minor anomalies compared to the actual plant, was confirmatively identified in a personal interview with Dr. Nicolas Hallé, Assistant-Director of the Laboratoire de Phanérogamie at Paris' Jardin des Plantes.—The *Dictionnaire de Baillon*, moreover, corroborates the fact that the artichoke was introduced into France in the sixteenth century.

The Labors of the Months

1. Recent studies of the Vendôme stalls have been published by Claude Bayle and Suzanne Trocmé in the 1968 and 1969 issues of *Bulletin de la Société Archéologique, Scientifique et Littéraire du Vendômois*.

2. The former abbey's landed riches and its patronal relations with its many subjects were outlined by A. Dupré in *Congrès Archéologiques*, 1872, pp. 292–7.

The Beast in Man

1. The basic source for the stalls of St-Pierre is the collection of documents published by C. Port in the *Revue des Sociétés Savantes des Départements*, VII, 1868. These documents give the complete information regarding the two teams of artists who worked on the stalls, the first on the basis of a contractual system of pay, the second being paid by the day. The carvers are all named and the total amount each received for the period of his work is specified. The men obtained, besides, a daily meal consisting of one plate, bread, and "white wine" and were rewarded with "some special good victuals on important holidays."

A State of Grace

1. Biographic data on Robert de Balsac are from the *Dictionnaire de biographie francaise*, IV, 1941, article by Roman d'Amat.

2. A copy of the original foundation document of the collegiate church is at the Bibliothèque de Clermont-Ferrand. It has been paraphrased by Paul Roudié in *Revue de la Haute-Auvergne*, 1958.

3. In trying to check the nationality of the St-Chamant misericord artist or artists, we consulted a number of sources and in particular a recent two-volume work by Jacqueline Boccador, *Statuaire médiévale en France de 1400 à 1530*, 1974, which reproduces many hundreds of sculptures of the period when St-Chamant's misericords were being carved. It must be said that there is little, if any, of this work that resembles the style or spirit of St-Chamant.

4. The collegiate church of St-Chamant was demolished in 1808 when it was still, reportedly, in perfect preservation. Happily, the stalls had already been moved out, part going to the village parish, the rest to two other churches in the vicinity, St-Cernin and St-Illide.

A Princess's Votive Offering

1. The Eglise de Brou is fairly completely documented in the departmental archives, a number of the documents having been published by Jules Finot in *Réunions des Sociétés des Beaux-Arts des Départements*, XII (1888), as well as by other authors. The most thorough historical account of the church's construction and of the life of its founder, Princess Margaret, is by Jules Baux, *Histoire de l'église de Brou*, 1854.

2. The figures of 250,000 *florins* was extrapolated by us from the fabric administrator's accounts of expenditures during the ten years of 1523 to 1532, which showed a total of 139,445 *florins* (J. Baux, p. 203, n. 1). A *florin* was worth about 80 percent of a *livre*.

3. No document, unfortunately, either identifies the person who was in charge of the construction of the stalls or any artist who worked on them; nor is there any firm date for their creation.

The Burghers' "Self"-Portraits

1. Jules Baux, in his *Notice descriptive et historique sur l'église collégiale de Notre-Dame-de-Bourg*, is again the best source for Bourg-en-Bresse's second most important structure. In his account, he often quotes at length from the original documents, mainly the *Registres Municipaux*. They are the origin, for example, of the report given in 1527 by the retiring head of the church fabric for his ten years' service, in which the total income is listed as 13,076 *florins*, 3 *gros*, and 7 *forts*.

2. The contract signed with the local carvers is recorded in the *Archives Communales,* BB 24, April 19, 1510.

A Lesson in Semantics

1. Actually, Jean de Vitry was a native Savoyard who had settled in Geneva early in life, where he had evidently learnt his profession of stall-building. Bernard Prost, archivist, published in 1877 a document of 1449 which reviewed the terms for the construction of the St-Claude stalls as arranged between "Jean de Vitry, bourgeois de Geneve," and Gales Vaucher, a burgher of St-Claude and churchwarden of its cathedral. We know that Jean de Vitry completed the stalls in 1465 from the inscription on his carved portrait on one of the terminal panels.

2. The 1576 plaque was identified in 1884 by Bernard Prost, who published the wording on it.

3. The account of the repair of the stalls by Robelin de Colonne, starting in 1869, was reported by A. Vayssiere in *Les stalles de la cathédrale de St-Claude,* 1874.

4. The identification of the preaching pig as Calvin (Fig. 107) is based on a misericord at the ancient church of St-Sernin in Toulouse, which shows a pig in the pulpit sermonizing three other pigs and bears the inscription: "Calvin, the pig, preaching."

The Entrepreneur of Stalls

1. André Sulpice's four major stalls were taken on by him one after the other, and he was directing most of them at the same time, their dates being: Chartreuse, 1461–1477; Loc-Dieu, 1469–?; Collégiale, 1473–1487; Rodez, 1478–1489.

2. The Rodez contract was published in full by Louis de Marlavagne in his *Histoire de la cathédrale de Rodez,* 1875. In it, Sulpice was guaranteed a block sum of 1,700 *livres tour.* (of Tours) from which he had to pay his seven assistants. The cathedral chapter agreed to supply him, his family, and the artists a house to live and work in, as well as grain, meat, and wine. It also furnished all building supplies, wood, nails, and glue.

3. The Collégiale stalls were approved after Sulpice showed the assembled consuls and canons a model or plan, according to the *Archives Communales* of Nov. 19, 1473, as quoted by Victor Lafon in his work on the stalls published in 1889.

4. The conflict between the consuls and clerics over the size of the Collégiale stalls is narrated in the early eighteenth-century manuscript history of the municipality which was published by Etienne Cabrol in 1860 under the title, *Annales de Villefranche-de-Rouergue.*

5. Loc-Dieu's stalls were bought by a pious confraternity in 1808 and turned over to the Pénitents-Noirs of Villefranche, where they can be seen today.

Created in Turmoil

1. The complete account of Rouen Cathedral's stalls can be gleaned from the departmental archives, under *Comptes de la Fabrique,* starting in 1457 (G. 2492), and in the *Acta in Capitulo* or *Délibérations Capitulaires,* starting with the register for 1451–1460 (G. 2135). The details have been inventorized in the *Inventaire-Sommaire des Archives Départementales,* Série G, Tome II, 1874. E. H. Langlois gave an excellent account of the basic information in his *Stalles de la cathédrale de Rouen,* 1838, with precious drawings of all the misericords, including the twenty-two that were destroyed in the 1944 bombing. Major patron of the stalls was Archbishop-Cardinal Guillaume d'Estouteville. Their total cost was 6,961 *livres, 12 sous, 5 deniers.*

2. Missions in search of carvers are listed for 1454, 1460/61, 1462 (twice), 1465/66 (twice), 1467/68.

3. Most Rouen carvers got five *sous* a day and were paid weekly. Hence, Mosselmen got the equivalent of one day's pay for a misericord, four days' pay for a larger statue. The pay of carvers in different places and periods varied considerably with the value of the *livre* and the *sou.* There were usually twenty *sous* to a *livre.*

4. The eighty-six misericords drawn by Langlois in 1838 (two of them had disappeared much earlier) are overwhelmingly secular, only fourteen of eighty-four identifiable subjects being religious. In contrast, there are no fewer than thirty-one work scenes and eleven from daily life.

Carvings from a Phantom Chapel

1. The epic of the wanderings of Gaillon's stalls has been traced by J. J. Marquet de Vasselot in *Bulletin Monumental,* 1927.

2. The *Comptes de dépenses de la construction du château de Gaillon,* published in 1850 by the archivist, A. Deville, is one of the most remarkable records of its kind. Its thousands of entries include names of artists, fees, dates, areas in which they worked, etc.

3. Though the Gaillon stalls were begun in 1508, sculpture was not undertaken until the following year, as we learn from the purchase of six "parchment skins" on which "pourtraicts" (drawings) for the stalls were to be sketched. We have no total figure for the cost of the stalls, but Colin Castille, their master-of-works, got 1,200 *livres* in partial payment for them in 1515/16 and a final payment of 100 *livres* in 1517/18, as recorded in the *Inventaire-Sommaire du Département de la Seine-Maritime,* Série G, 1866.

4. The abbott's throne, the sole St-Lucien remnant now left at St-Denis, was quite apparently freely worked over in the nineteenth century.

5. The story of the making of the stalls of the Abbey of St-Lucien-près-Beauvais, most of whose carvings can be seen at Paris's Cluny Museum, is told by L.-E. Deladreue et Mathon in the *Mémoires de la Société Académique d'Archéologie, Sciences et Arts . . . de l'Oise,* 1871, and by various other authors.

The "Grammar of Classicism"

1. The outstanding reference for both sets of stalls is the doctoral thesis of Mathilde Villotte devoted to French choir-stalls in southern France, *La Renaissance et un groupe de stalles du midi,* 1930.

2. The contract between Pietro Ghinucci and Dominique Bertin of Toulouse for the terminal work on the Auch stalls was discovered and published in 1896 by Célestin Douais (*Les stalles du choeur de Ste-Marie d'Auch*). Dated March 15, 1552, it is the sole document that we have on these stalls and it is a very partial one. The contract ran for only two years and Bertin received 1,700 *livres,* which undoubtedly included pay for other workers, in addition to lodging, the wood and other materials likewise being furnished by the church.

A Conscientious Prelate's Message

1. Major source of information about Bishop Jacques Amyot and his prelacy at Auxerre is Jean Lebeuf, France's outstanding eighteenth-century church archivist and historian (*Mémoires concernant l'histoire civile et ecclésiastique d'Auxerre et de son ancien diocèse,* edition of 1848/55; also his *Histoire de la prise d'Auxerre par les Huguenots . . . 1567–1568,* 1723). Many of the documents Lebeuf quotes as sources have disappeared.

2. Misericords with New Testament subjects collated by us were found in only ten churches. Besides those at Auxerre and *St-Sulpice-de-Favières,* the church of Lorris has seven and Auch Cathedral four. The six other churches have but one New Testament subject each.

A Proud City's Pageant Play

1. Amiens's stalls have been studied and documented in two excellent works: Louis Jourdain and A.-T. Duval, *Les stalles de la cathédrale d'Amiens,* 1843, and Georges Durand, *Monographie de l'église Notre-Dame, cathédrale d'Amiens,* Tome II, 1903. These authors record all the available secondary material that furnishes whatever we know about the names of artists, dates of their functioning, cost of the stalls, and known donors. The stalls were begun in July 1508 and probably completed in 1519. Originally there were 120 stalls but 10 were removed at two different times to gain space.

2. Both Huet and Boulin earned 4 *sous* a day but each got a yearly bonus of 12 *écus,* or 288 *sous,* which raised their pay to about 5 *sous* daily. An ordinary carver at Amiens earned 3.

3. Antoine Avernier's role as carver of the misericords appears in a manuscript of the Bibliothèque d'Amiens, Ms. 517, p. 40. The reason for our reservation expressed in the text is the high pay he was said to receive—32 *sous*—for each carving, as compared to Pol Mosselmen's pay at Rouen Cathedral of 5 *sous.* It must be said, however, that Amiens's misericords are more complex than Rouen's, with many more figures and finer detail.

4. For the important contributions of the powerful Amiens municipality to the cathedral's art, see Henry Kraus's "The Medieval Commune of Amiens as Patron of Art and Architecture," in the *Gazette des Beaux-Arts,* December 1971.

5. Georges Durand suggests as the source of the Joseph imagery in the Amiens misericords the vignettes in a popular contemporary book of hours by Simon Vostre and Antoine Vérard.

Apotheosis of the Object

1. The Abbé Truchet, a local scholar, gathered material about the cathedral over many years and published a part of it in 1887, in his *St-Jean-de-Maurienne au 16e siècle*. He also studied St-Jean's guilds and confraternities as well as the organization of the municipal council. The city and part of the church had to be repaired after a big flood that took place around 1440. Archbishop Guillaume d'Estouteville, chief patron of Rouen's stalls, who had added the post of Bishop of St-Jean to his other dignities in 1453, was responsible for much of the restorative work undertaken at Maurienne. It was his successor, Etienne de Morel, however, who built the new choir and had stalls carved for it, hiring for the task another Geneva artist, Pierre Mochet, a contemporary of Jean de Vitry, though another author, Robert Berton, maintains that there is no document certifying that Mochet, *carpentator ymaginum*, created these stalls (*Les stalles de l'insigne collégiale de St-Pierre et de St-Ours d'Aoste*, 1964). The cost of St-Jean's stalls was 2,086 *florins*, according to a chronicle published around 1670 and cited by Abbé Truchet.

MISERICORDS OF OTHER COUNTRIES

Great Britain

1. A list of stall dates was assembled by Francis Bond in his book cited under the *Foreword* notes. Some additions and clarifications were made by later scholars. In particular, George L. Druce in an article in *Jour. Brit. Arch. Assoc.*, 1931, studied the changing form of the seat ledge, the wing sculpture and other details as dating indices. British stall dates were also collated by G. L. Remnant from a great variety of sources in his *Catalogue*.

Belgium

2. Bond's quotation is from his cited work. Yet this scholar was himself prompt to indicate places where Flemish (and other) influences had impinged on English carving.

3. In Louis Maeterlinck's book (cited in the *Foreword* notes), he devotes large sections in trying to prove the existence of Flemish artists or borrowings from their works by sculptors of other countries. Despite his exaggerations, the fact remains that Flemish influences in stall-art were widespread. Flanders carvers were documented at Rouen Cathedral, for example, and other French churches where their imprint is felt are Champeaux, St-Martin-aux-Bois, Eglise de Brou, Bordeaux's St-Seurin, Paris's St-Gervais and others.

4. The earliest of Belgium's seven leading sets are Bruges's St-Sauveur (c. 1430) and Louvain's St-Pierre (1438–42), Hoogstraten's Ste-Catherine the latest (1546).

5. An important recent work on Belgian choir-stalls is by J. K. Steppe, *Wereld van Vroomheid en Satire*, 1973.

Germany

6. We checked the old stalls of a dozen churches in south Germany, finding misericords in only two of them: Ulm and Constance.

7. A derivative role for German misericords was suggested by two of their authors, specialists in the subject: Fritz Neugass, *Studien zur deutschen Kunstgeschichte: Mittelalterliches Chorgestühl in Deutschland*, 1927, and Hannelore Sachs, *Mittelalterliches Chorgestühl von Erfurt bis Stralsund*, 1964, a book devoted chiefly to work in East Germany.

8. Ulm's stalls are discussed and handsomely illustrated in one of Langewiesche-Bücherei's popular series of art monographs, the author being Hans Seifert, the photographer Erich Müller-Cassel.

Switzerland

9. Paul L. Ganz's work, published in 1946, is titled *Das Chorgestühl in der Schweiz*. The majority of the nearly two hundred stalls listed by him are from the seventeenth–nineteenth centuries, with only sixty-five stemming from the earlier period.

10. Robert Berton, in his already cited work, points to the important fact that when the thirteen "Gothic stalls" were created, Swiss political and cultural penetration spread into Upper Swabia, Alsace, Burgundy, and Savoy.

One Hundred Important French Misericord Collections

LOCATED IN FIFTY-FOUR DIFFERENT DEPARTMENTS

THIRTEENTH CENTURY: Notre-Dame-de-la-Roche (Yvelines); Poitiers Cathedral (Vienne).

FOURTEENTH CENTURY: Chaise-Dieu (Haute-Loire); Dol-de-Bretagne (Ille-et-Vilaine); Lisieux, St-Pierre (Calvados).

FIFTEENTH CENTURY: Abondance (Haute-Savoie); Albi Cathedral (Tarn); Béhuard (Maine-et-Loire); Blainville-Crevon (Seine-Maritime); Bommiers (Indre); Bordeaux, St-Seurin (Gironde); Bourth (Eure); Cerisy-la-Forêt (Manche); Chezal-Benoît (Cher); Embrun (Hautes-Alpes); Evian-les-Bains (Haute-Savoie); Flavigny-sur-Ozerain (Côte-d'Or); Isle-Adam (Val-d'Oise); Jarze' (Maine-et-Loire); Lautenbach (Haut-Rhin); Les Andelys, Notre-Dame (Eure); Mortemart (Haute-Vienne); Paris, Cluny Museum; Prey (Eure); Rodez Cathedral (Aveyron); Rouen Cathedral (Seine-Maritime); Routot (Eure); St-Cernin and St-Chamant (Cantal); St-Claude Cathedral (Jura); St-Illide (Cantal); St-Jean-de-Maurienne Cathedral (Savoie); St-Léonard-de-Noblat (Haute-Vienne); St-Martin-aux-Bois (Oise); St-Sulpice-de-Favières (Essonne); Saumur, St-Pierre (Maine-et-Loire); Solignac (Haute-Vienne); Thann (Haut-Rhin); Vendôme, La Trinité (Loir-et-Cher); Villefranche-de-Rouergue: La Collégiale, La Chartreuse and Les Pénitents-Noirs (Aveyron); Villiers-sur-Loir (Loir-et-Cher).

SIXTEENTH CENTURY: Amiens Cathedral (Somme); Auch Cathedral (Gers); Auxerre Cathedral (Yonne); Barjols (Var); Besse-en-Chandesse (Puy-de-Dôme); Boos (Seine-Maritime); Bourg-en-Bresse: Eglise de Brou and La Collégiale (Ain); Castelnau-Magnoac (Hautes-Pyrénées); Champeaux (Seine-et-Marne); Château de Mailleraye-sur-Seine (Seine-Maritime); Chaumont-en-Vexin (Oise); Conlie (Sarthe); Dax Cathedral (Landes); Estouteville-Ecalles (Seine-Maritime); Gassicourt, Mantes-la-Jolie (Yvelines); Goupillieres (Eure); Guerche-de-Bretagne (Ille-et-Vilaine); Herbault (Loir-et-Cher); Le Mans Cathedral (Sarthe); Les Bottereaux (Eure); Levroux (Indre); Lorris (Loiret); Maurs (Cantal); Montbenoît (Doubs); Montréal (Yonne); Mortain (Manche); Nègrepelisse (Tarn-et-Garonne); Orbais (Marne); Ormes (Eure); Paris, St-Gervais; Pont-Ste-Marie (Aube); Pont-St-Pierre (Eure); Ponts-de-Cé (Maine-et-Loire); Presles (Val-d'Oise); Puy-Notre-Dame (Maine-et-Loire); St-Bertrand-de-Comminges (Haute-Garonne); St-Denis, Basilique (Seine-St-Denis); St-Epain (Indre-et-Loire); St-Papoul (Aude); St-Pierre-sur-Dives (Calvados); St-Pol-de-Léon (Nord-Finistere); Soignolles (Seine-et-Marne); Solesmes (Sarthe); Tréguier Cathedral (Côtes-du-Nord); Villabé (Essonne).

SEVENTEENTH CENTURY: Abbaye de Chancelade (Dordogne); Caen, St-Etienne (Calvados); Moissac (Tarn-et-Garonne); Moutier-d'Ahun (Creuse); Moyenmoutier (Vosges); Oiron (Deux-Sèvres); Sarlat (Dordogne); Soissons Cathedral (Aisne); Toulouse: Cathedral and St-Sernin (Haute-Garonne); Viviers Cathedral (Ardèche).

Misericords
of
France

Amiéns

Estouteville
Mailleraye · Blainville · St-Maffin-Bois
Rouen · Soissons
Routot · Boos
Cerisy-la-Forêt · Pont-St-P. · Chaumont-en-V.
Caën · Andelys · Isle-Adam
St-Pierre/D. · Liseux · Goupillières · Gassi- · Presles
· Ormes · court · St-Denis
· Prey
Tréguier · Les Bottereaux · Orbais
St-Pol-de-Léon · Bourth · PARIS(2)
· Dol-de-B. · Mortain · N-D-de-La-Roche
· Villabé · Soignolles
· St-Sulpice-de-F. · Champeaux
Pont-Ste-Marie · Moyenmoutier
Conlie · Lautenbach
Guerche-de-B. · Thann
Solesmes · Le Mans
Villiers/Loir · Vendôme · Lorris · Auxerre
· Jarzé · Herbault · Montréal
Béhuard · Flavigny
Ponts-de-Cé · Saumur
Puy-Notre-Dame · St-Epain · Montbenoît
· Oiron · Levroux
· Chézal-Benoît · St-Claude · Evian
Poitiers · Bommiers · Abondance
· Bourg-en-
Bresse(2)
· Mortemart · Moutier-d'Ahun
· St-Léonard-de-N.
· Solignac · St-Jean-de-
Besse-en-Chandesset · Maurienne
Chancelade · Chaise-Dieu
St-Cernin · Embrun
St-Chamant
Sarlat · St-Illide · Viviers
Bordeaux · Maurs
Villefranche(3)
Rodez
Moissac
Nègrepelisse
· Albi
· Dax · Auch · Barjols
· Toulouse(2)
Castelnau-M. · St-Papoul
· St-Bertrand-de-C.